GOD'S
GENTLE
WHISPER

by Denise George

AGLOW®
PUBLICATIONS

A Ministry of Women's Aglow Fellowship, Int'l.
P.O. Box 1548
Lynnwood, WA 98046-1548
USA

Cover design by David Marty

Suggested Subject Heading: Prayer/Christian Living

Women's Aglow Fellowship, International is a non-denominational organization of Christian women. Our mission is to lead women to Jesus Christ and provide opportunity for Christian women to grow in their faith and minister to others.

Aglow Publications is the publishing ministry of Women's Aglow Fellowship, Int'l. Our publications are used to help women find a personal relationship with Jesus Christ, to enhance growth in their Christian experience, and to help them recognize their roles and relationship according to Scripture.

For more information about Women's Aglow Fellowship, please write to Women's Aglow Fellowship, Int'l., P.O. Box 1548, Lynnwood, WA 98046-1548, USA, or call (206) 775-7282.

Unless otherwise noted, all scripture quotations in this publication are from the Holy Bible, New International Version. Copyright © 1973, 1978, 1984, International Bible Society. Other versions abbreviated as follows: NCV (New Century Version), NKJV (New King James Version), RSV (Revised Standard Version), KJV (King James Version).

ISBN 1-56616-001-4

1 2 3 4 5 6 7 8 9 10 Printing / Year 97 96 95 94 93

GOD'S GENTLE WHISPER

The Lord said,
"Go out and stand on the mountain
in the presence of the Lord,
for the Lord is about to pass by."

Then a great and powerful wind
tore the mountains apart
and shattered the rocks before the Lord,
but the Lord was not in the wind.

After the wind there was an earthquake,
but the Lord was not in the earthquake.

After the earthquake came a fire,
but the Lord was not in the fire.

And after the fire came a *gentle whisper.*

When Elijah heard it,
he pulled his cloak over his face
and went out and stood at the mouth of the cave

(I Kings 19:11-13).

DEDICATION

For
Terry Helwig
and
Helen Parker
friends forever

Preface and Acknowledgments

I am excited about this book on prayer! During the years I spent praying over it, researching it, and pondering the whole idea of prayer, God has enriched my own personal prayer life in ways I never thought possible. I have discovered a new joy both for the quiet times of prayer retreat as well as the busy day's "prayers on the run." Prayer is, without a doubt, an exciting discovery, an incredible adventure.

I thank God for providing this opportunity to put my heart-felt words on paper. And I thank the editorial staff at Aglow Publications for making the sharing of these words with you a reality. My prayer is that in some way God will use this book to touch your hearts in new, vibrant, inspiring ways for Him.

❧

Needless to say, writing a book is a task I cannot do alone.

My sincere gratitude goes to Dr. Ernest C. Reisinger, theologian and friend, who supplied me with outstanding out-of-print materials on the subject of prayer, and who encouraged this project from its conception.

My thanks also go to two special friends and fellow writers whose judgment I respect, and whose time and energy spent on the pages of this book I appreciate: clinical counselor, Dr. Ray Burwick and educator, Dr. Carolyn Tomlin.

A word of thanksgiving must be said to my devoted pastor, Dr. Charles Carter, whose friendship I treasure, and whose messages keep me inspired.

A word of appreciation also must be said to my parents, Bob and Willene Wyse, the most wonderful dad and mom a person could have. Thank you for listening to my dreams, for encouraging me during a dozen years of writing, and for loving me (in spite of me!).

My gratitude to you, my friends who have prayed for this project. I have felt the strength of your prayers in every word written.

And, as always, my admiration, my adoration, and my appreciation to the three who know me best—and still love me anyway: My husband, Dr. Timothy George, and my children, Christian, 11, and Alyce Elizabeth, 9.

Note: Before you begin reading *God's Gentle Whisper*, it would be helpful to reread the fascinating story of the prophet Elijah, found in I Kings 17, 18, and 19.

May I also recommend that you read this book aloud in a quiet place and that you pause frequently throughout its pages as the Holy Spirit leads you to ponder and to pray.

GOD'S GENTLE WHISPER

As a Christian woman
I believe our life's goal is
to know God
to love God
and
to serve God.
We come to know God, to love God, and to serve God
through prayer.
But prayer is not only speaking our words to Him,
singing and dancing, and raising our hands.
Prayer is also finding a quiet place
and with the ears of seeking hearts
waiting and listening for God's gentle whisper to us.
For . . .
When we learn to listen with the ears of our hearts,
we come to know God.
When we hear His gentle whisper,
we come to love God.
And when to His whisper our listening hearts respond,
we prepare to serve God.

Contents

Section I

The Waiting Heart

(When we learn to listen with the ears of our hearts,
we come to know God.)

The Lord said,
"Go out and stand on the mountain
in the presence of the Lord,
for the Lord is about to pass by"
(I Kings 19:1).

1

...

Standing on the Mountain: The Secret Place

While my young son plays quietly in the next room, I sit beside my grandmother's bed and hold her trembling hand. Beneath the layers of handmade quilts, I see the frail woman I call "Mama," the woman I have loved dearly for more than three decades.

Alice Crane Williams, my beloved grandmother, Mama, is dying. I cannot imagine life without her.

She is a simple woman who has suffered a lifetime of sickness and surgery. In her eighty years, she has never written a check, never driven a car, and never worked outside her home.

She would not rate very high on the world's yardstick of accomplishment. Yet, I know few women who have accomplished more. She has lived a long life in step with her

Lord, empowered by the Holy Spirit, devoted to discipleship. Her spiritual impact on others has been profound. As my spiritual mother, she has left an indelible fingerprint of love and grace and beauty on my life.

A WELCOME HAVEN

A storm brews outside her home, the white gabled house I have known since my birth. Dark clouds appear and are followed by bouts of thunder and lightning. The wind begins snapping off young trees at their roots and tossing them into the yard.

I expect to hear my son scream out with fear as I glance out the window into nature's chaos. Yet, however frightening the scene beyond these walls, inside we feel safe, secure, unafraid. The house is a welcome haven from the turmoil all around us.

Mama and I are not alone in the room where I so often slept as a child. For within me is nestled one still in development, one who will carry on my grandmother's name. My unborn daughter, Alyce, remains peaceful in her secret place beneath my heart. It is as if she somehow senses the preciousness of this moment for Mama and me, our moment of timelessness, our moment of unspoken prayer together in our own secret place.

Will Mama live to look upon the face of her new great-granddaughter, her only namesake? I wonder as greater darkness and the threat of more severe storms shadow the room.

I already seem to know the answer.

No, she won't. Mama will close her eyes and cease her breathing just ten days before Alyce will open her eyes and take her first breath of life.

This is our last meeting. Our final face-to-face farewell. And with the birth so close, I won't be able to travel the long distance to her funeral. We both sense we will meet again only in the promised life hereafter.

So many times I have made the 300-mile trek to sit by my grandmother's side. Like little girls at a slumber party, we have talked and giggled and dreamed about the future. And how the minutes flew! We looked at our watches as if staring hard enough at them would make time slow down. But, alas, each time, the sun rose, I rolled up my sleeping bag, packed my pajamas, said my thank-yous, and returned to my busy world far away from Mama's world.

Mama and I have loved our many times of nonstop conversation. But today, in Mama's short meantime between life and death, in this time of quiet waiting, we do not speak. We need no words. And in this secret place, our paradise away from the thundering world outside, we sense the presence of Another who waits with us.

❧

There are times in our lives so deep, so precious, so near to the core of our hearts, that words only hinder our communion. Thus it is with prayer. Our hearts can be so full of love or pain or gratitude or fear that our very silence overflows with meaning beyond the limited capability of words. We express ourselves instead with the prayer that pours forth from a touched heart, a heart so sensitive to its own beat that words would be bumbling.

"The fewer words the better prayer," said Martin Luther.

On this night, this storm-raged night when death glares at us from down the hall, I would agree with Mr. Luther. Words need be sparse. Our clasped hands, smiling eyes, and memories of a life lived side by side, say more than we ever could. Words would make a clumsy stab at what our hearts so eloquently express.

GOD'S WHISPER

"But thou, when thou prayest, enter into thy closet, and when thou hast shut thy door, pray to thy Father which is in secret. . . ."[1]

"Thy Father which is in secret. . . ." Mama has spent much time in closet-prayer secreted with the Father. In fact, her entire life has been a prayer. More than anyone else, Mama has taught me the value and beauty of a secret place and a prayer of waiting and listening to the still, small voice that whispers within the prayer-closet walls.

One of my favorite authors, C. S. Lewis, believed that "God whispers to us in our pleasures, . . . but shouts in our pain: it is His megaphone," he writes, "to rouse a deaf world."[2]

Dare I disagree with C. S. Lewis?

I would reverse the order. For I believe it is in our times of pleasure that God must shout and rouse our deaf ears. Pleasure often dulls our sense of need for God. Truly, it is in our pain that He need only whisper. For in our pain the deaf ears of our hearts are unstopped, waiting, listening, hanging onto the comfort of His every word. Pain, the Great Teacher, can break our hearts and cause us to contemplate deeply humankind's most pondered question: "Why, Lord, why?"

There is but one Theologian who knows the answer. Thus, to Him we turn our hearts and yearn for deeper understanding.

❧

Waiting. Watching. Listening. There are many wonderful and beautiful ways to pray, to communicate with the Father. But it is the prayer that waits and watches, the prayer that perks the ears of our hearts to strain and to listen expectantly for God's gentle whisper, that compels me to record it. For this waiting, this "standing under, in active strength, enduring till the answer comes,"[3] describes prayer at its richest.

I have discovered an abundant love for this type of prayer, the prayer of the waiting heart. Perhaps you, too, have discovered its surprising beauty and lasting afterglow.

❦

I used to think of waiting as a passive activity. I have felt time wasting as I've stood in long, grocery check-out lines, bank lines, cafeteria lines, post office lines. I loathe that kind of waiting where I must persist staring into space with mind wandering. But waiting in prayer is nothing like waiting in line. It is far from a passive activity.

When God's great and beloved prophet, Elijah, waited for God on the side of the mountain, he did not passively sit or lie or lounge in his waiting. He had no blank stare and wandering mind. Elijah *stood* on the mountain, actively waiting, his eyes alert and watchful, his ears perked and eager to detect God's voice.

Over the past few years, Elijah has taught me much about how to pray this way. Elijah and Mama.

MAMA'S SECRET PLACE

Oh, that I could know God as Elijah and Mama knew him!

On a cool spring morning, long before the pet rooster summoned us to rise, I looked from the kitchen window, beyond the tall hickory nut trees, to the gardens that bloomed in bounty each year. Mama's flower gardens. Mama's secret place to meet the Lord.

I am sure her gardens brought more than one passerby to prayer. So lovely, they lined the small farm's edge.

19

People often stopped and admired them for a few rare moments of hushed beauty. And there in the midst of dew-laden blooms, Mama slowly walked. At times she lingered, her lips moving in silent prayer. Most times, however, her lips were still. She touched a treasured rose, and then with eyes moist from an overflowing heart, she simply looked toward the heavens and smiled.

Mama needed no words to commune with her Father. For they had walked through the gardens many times together, their hearts beating as one in perfect peace and communion.

❧

Do you have a secret place, a place where you go alone to wait and watch and listen for the Lord? A place where you go faithfully to know your Father more intimately?

God is a God who wants to be known.[4] We wait, we watch, we listen, and God rewards our seeking with knowledge of Himself.[5] J. I. Packer, in his book *Knowing God* writes that the greatest gift God gives us is the gift of knowing Him.[6] Imagine! We can actually know the one who created us, the one who knew us in our mother's womb long before we drew our first breath and opened our eyes to His glorious creation.

❧

I have had many secret places over the years, places where I have spent quiet precious moments with the Lord. Some places were lovely to the eye and peaceful to the heart.

I remember the little private spot hidden by trees on a tall mountain in Rüschlikon, Switzerland, the "village of the roses." It became my secret place of worship for almost a year.

Standing on the Mountain: The Secret Place

I often stood on the side of the mountain in the pinestraw nest powdered with fresh snow, and tried to absorb the incomprehensible beauty. The emerald and shimmering gold Lake Zurich lay directly below me, the forests of snow-laden evergreens surrounded me, and the mighty Alps rose in distant peaks beyond me. It seemed right out of a storybook. I often blinked my eyes to believe the exquisite scenery before me.

On this, my own Elijah's mountain, I stood silently, my mouth agape in awe of the Creator's masterpiece. I believed no place in the world could be more breathtakingly beautiful.

Waiting? Yes.

Watching? Definitely.

Listening? With all the strength I could summon.

There, I waited in my own secret place, with expectation and a seeking heart, waiting for the Lord to pass by.

AN INNER CITY SECRET PLACE

In sharp contrast to Rüschlikon, with its rose petal fragrance lingering in the air, was another of my many secret places: Chelsea, Massachusetts, a dirty, violent, inner city located on the outskirts of Boston.

It was a far cry from Rüschlikon with its Sleeping Beauty setting. In storybook language, Chelsea would be more like Alice in Wonderland with its dangerous pathways, unpredictable curves, and its strange assortment of characters hiding behind every wall. A storm of violence, pain, and suffering rained heavily on the 30,000 Chelsea residents of all colors, ages, and backgrounds, who lived crowded into two square miles of drab city concrete. We did not choose Chelsea. We are drawn to and inspired by mountains and trees and sparkling lakes. Chelsea was chosen for us by the mission board of our denomination.

Indeed, Chelsea was a mission field. It proved a seven-year missionary experience I will never forget.

Chelsea had no sweet rose fragrance. Its only beauty lived in the innocent and loving faces of those too young to yet be aware of its poverty.

There was the unwed mother with eleven children living in the one-room attic of a four-story apartment building.

There were the alcoholics who lived in the drainage ditch with no food and no hope.

There were gangs of teens drinking and drifting through the late night streets with no direction, no guidance, no future outside prison walls.

And there were the children, the children of the concrete city. Children like David, who was placed in an abusive foster home as a baby. David coped with life as no child should ever have to.

We tried to adopt David, the five-year-old boy who had never seen a real flower push its way through dirt. But we were unsuccessful. I often wonder where he is now, the dark-skinned boy with bruises on his back and a little round face that seldom smiled.

In Rüschlikon my heart was filled with prayers of thanksgiving for the beauty that surrounded and inspired me. I needed few words to express the gratitude of my heart.

In Chelsea, however, my heart was filled with prayers for others, the crowds of people who tried to survive hard days surrounded by drugs, prostitution, and desolation. I needed few words to express the pain in my heart for the poverty and suffering that surrounded me. Intercessory prayer from my heart repeatedly asked the "whys" of faith, the hard questions—questions for which I waited and watched and strained to hear the answers.

In Chelsea, my secret place was a ladder-back chair at an enamel-painted table before a window that looked out on filth and vulgar depravity. But however unsettling the view, I found I was drawn much more to wait in prayer at that kitchen table than on that mountain in Rüschlikon, so great was my need to listen for God's voice in the midst of such fear and suffering.

God needed no megaphone to rouse my deaf ears. I lived in Chelsea for only a few years. But these people would live there forever. In the pain I felt for them, I listened attentively, carefully for His comforting whisper and the answers I needed to hear.

BACK INTO THE STORM

It is time for me to leave my grandmother's quiet bedroom. For the last time, I lean over and lightly kiss her forehead. I would speak one last time to Mama by phone, but I would never see her again.

"I'll see you later, Mama," are the only words I speak.

We look into each other's eyes and we smile. We both know what *later* means. I stand and back slowly out of the room, taking one last mental snapshot to hold in memory throughout my life without her. Through intense physical pain, she keeps the smile on her lips until the loving embrace of our eyes is broken by distance.

As I leave our secret place, I am once again aware of the storm outside. I lift my small son from his playpen, and together we brace the wind and rain and leave the house that will never be the same to me again.

❧

Every heart must have its hush. I am convinced that the waiting prayer is the most difficult prayer to pray. In our lives, it is often much easier to *do* than it is to *be*, to pray with words and song and joyful dance than to wait and listen in sacred solitude. Yet the Lord summons us to go out and stand on our mountaintop, to *"be* still, and *know* that I am God."[7]

Our hearts are forever searching for a quiet place of solitude, a secret place where they alone can prepare us for an encounter with the living Lord.

QUESTIONS FOR GROUP STUDY

1. Have you personally known the richness of a spiritual nurturer in your life? If so, describe that person.
   – What qualities made her/him different from others you loved and respected?
   – What traits did she/he possess that spoke to you in spiritually-inspiring ways?
   – How did that person bring you closer to the Lord?
   – What is the one most important spiritual lesson you learned from your nurturer?

2. What does this sentence mean to you: "Our hearts can be so full of love or pain or gratitude or fear that our very silence overflows with meaning beyond the limited capability of words"?
   – Have you ever prayed so deeply from your heart that words only got in your way? Describe the event. What was your life situation when you prayed that particular prayer?

3. Do you agree with Martin Luther: "The fewer words the better prayer"? If so, explain.

4. What does Scripture teach when it states: "But thou, when thou prayest, enter into thy closet, and when thou hast shut thy door, pray to thy Father which is in secret. . . ."?[8]

– Why is it important that we have a secret place to pray, a private prayer-closet?

– What is the significance of the statement: "When thou hast shut thy door. . . ."?

– Do you have a secret place of prayer where you and the Father can regularly meet? Describe it.

– Why do you think a secret place is important to your life of prayer?

5. Do you agree that: "It is in our times of pleasure that God must shout and rouse our deaf ears," and that "It is in our pain that He need only whisper"? If so, why? If not, why?

6. Oswald Chambers describes *waiting* as "standing under, in active strength, enduring till the answer comes." Do you disagree with his definition? If so, what does *waiting* mean to you?

7. Describe your most beautiful secret place. What quali ties did it have, or does it now have, that move you most to prayer?

8. "I am convinced that the waiting prayer is the most difficult prayer to pray. It is often much easier to *do* than it is to *be*, to pray with words and song and joyful dance than to wait and listen with sacred solitude." Do you agree that "the waiting prayer" is the most difficult prayer to pray? Please explain why.

9. What are your five greatest strengths and your five greatest weaknesses in your pursuit of prayer? List them in order and discuss.

SUGGESTIONS FOR PERSONAL REFLECTION

Choose a favorite place in your home or garden or office or city park.

– Decide to visit your secret place at least once a day, if not more often.

– Give yourself time to sit quietly and to relax your body and mind.

– Read favorite selections from Scripture to help you focus more fully on the Lord.

– Pour out your heart to God. Keep nothing from Him.

– Then, listen. Listen as He speaks to the depths of your heart.

– Please do not rush this prayer-closet time, for it takes time to settle down and to totally concentrate on God, His love, His goodness. It takes time to prepare our hearts to hear His whisper.

– Schedule a time when you will be uninterrupted. Think only about God and His presence, and try to keep your thoughts from distractions. Concentrate on meeting the Lord and listening to His words to you.

2
...

The Seeking Heart

Hot, thirsty, and standing on aching feet, the man answers a deluge of questions—life and death questions—shouted to Him from a throng of people. They strain their ears to hear His answers in the push and shove of the sweaty crowd. Like bath sponges thrown into a vast ocean, they absorb all they can hold, yet they still thirst for more.

Lost coins, new wineskins, vines and branches . . . what did it all mean?

The preacher has been telling stories and explaining metaphors for hours without a coffee break. Some friends bring Him a burger and fries, but with the horde swarming around Him, demanding His time, He is unable to eat.

His throat is parched and He is bone tired, His voice cracks and fades into the lakeside wind.

27

"Speak louder! Speak louder! We can't hear you!" the multitudes demand in unison.

He turns and glances to the mountains on the other side of the lake. A voice beckons Him to come, a call more urgent than the clamor of the crowd.

"C'mon." He motions to his friends. "Let's find a quiet place to be alone and get some rest."

"But . . . but. . . ."

(Can't you just hear His friends' comments?)

"Now? Leave now? You've got to be kidding! This is the biggest revival we've ever had. You can't just 'drop out' in the middle of a sermon!"

They protest. He simply walks away, toward a little boat that will take Him toward the mountaintop, the secret place His heart seeks, the place where He can rest in the presence of the one who loves Him most.

Eyes set on the mountain, heart set on a respite, He rows to the other side of the lake.

"Surprise!" Like a child's surprise birthday party, the unexpected mob suddenly jumps out at Him, surrounding Him.

"Move aside!" someone shouts. "Let Him through! Tell us, more, man! P-l-e-a-s-e tell us more!"

"Speak louder! Speak louder! We can't hear you!" they demand.

The man rubs His tired eyes, takes a deep breath, and then lifts His head. He looks into the faces of the people who eagerly wait before Him, people with empty eyes and desperate hearts, people dying of spiritual thirst. They are like a herd of sheep wandering aimlessly through life with no guidance, no direction, no shepherd.

He leans against a rock for support, clears His throat, and parts His sun-baked lips to form words.

"The kingdom of God is like a mustard seed . . . ," He begins.

His stories last long into the evening. Before the sun disappears behind the mountains, before fatigue folds his legs beneath Him, Jesus will have filled hungry bellies with fish and loaves, and thirsty hearts with living water.

HE'S LIVED HERE

Jesus knows how it feels to be hot and thirsty and have aching feet. He knows the pressure of having more to do than can be humanly done in a single day. Jesus dealt with the crowds of demanding, critical people who believed of Him the worst and asked of Him the impossible. He knew time ticking away, the frustrations of ungrateful friends and family. He knew the pain of blistered hands, swollen eyes, and a hurting heart.

He's lived here, here in this stressful, pressure-packed Burger King society that hasn't really changed that much in 2000 years.

How did He endure it? Or, as we would put it in the twentieth century, how did He cope? How did He find rest and peace and tranquility and meaning in the midst of a thunder and lightning world? Where was His safe and secure haven when the storms of life gathered around Him?

On the mountaintop, His secret place, the place where He journeyed to meet His Father. Our Father.

Jesus spent much time on the mountaintops. When the crowds were at their biggest, when the pressures were at their greatest, He simply headed toward the nearest mountain. He made no excuses, He felt no guilt. When He heard the Father's call, He followed.

Right in the middle of a sermon.

He would have no qualms about leaving dirty dishes in the sink, the checkbook unbalanced, the family room floor unvacuumed. Prayer time with the Father was more important. It was the first item on His list of priorities.

29

Don't you just love a person like that, a person who has the courage to exit the ordinary to enter the extraordinary—a quiet, restful moment spent with God?

Think about it. If Jesus so needed to go to the mountaintop to be with the Father, far from the madding crowds, the pressures, the stresses of everyday life and work; if Jesus so needed to retreat, to pray, and to ponder, how much more do you and I need to take that hike.

Often.

Have you been to the mountaintop lately?

A LITTLE PEACE AND QUIET

Several Christmases ago, my then three-year-old son, Christian, asked me: "Mommy, what you want for 'Krismas?"

My husband, Timothy, and I were taking our study/ writing sabbatical that year in Switzerland. It was the best of times; it was the worst of times. Timothy and I were both under rigid book deadlines, we were both struggling to communicate in Swiss/German, and we were both trying (unsuccessfully) to potty train two preschoolers! We lived on a major four-lane highway, in an apartment the size of a postage stamp, with fourteen other international families—and one washing machine for us all.

What did I want for Christmas? Like the little boy who only wanted his two front teeth, I, too, had only two items on my gift list.

"All I want for Christmas, Christian," I answered, "is a little peace and quiet."

❦

Have you ever felt that way? Have you ever felt like a pitcher of water that has been poured out for others until it is bone dry?

I have. I find I need a lot of quiet, personal time with the Father in order to deal with the complexities of life and work and family and friends.

I believe Jesus felt that way, too. In fact, I'm glad he made so many recorded treks to the mountains. For his constant retreats give us an example. We are allowed to admit that our bodies grow tired and our hearts are in need of a quiet place where we can be alone with the Father.

Without excuses.

Without guilt.

Prayerful peace and quiet. It is a precious gift that no amount of money can buy. It is a free gift, a gift from God. And, high on the mountaintop, he waits for us, gift in hand, waiting to help us unwrap it.

A WISH GRANTED

Timothy overheard my request for peace and quiet on that Christmas several years ago. Early that Christmas morning, my wish was granted. From my family I received an envelope "filled with peace and quiet"—a three-day personal prayer retreat anywhere I wanted to go.

I chose the quietest place in all of Europe, a large twelfth-century stone monastery at the top of a mountain in Kappal, Switzerland. I spent those days and nights in silence, communing only with God and with the brown and white cows that chewed cud on the hillside.

During the day, I hiked the mountain trails, stopping to touch tender snow-dusted pine needles on lakeside evergreens and running my fingers across the smooth worn surfaces of roadside rocks. At night, I lay very still in my small room and listened to the soft distant chime of Swiss cowbells. I closed my eyes and tried to imagine all the many people who, for hundreds of years, had also waited quietly, prayerfully, in this place. At times, I even thought

31

God's Gentle Whisper

I heard the swish of a long robe worn by some ancient monk as he passed through the sacred halls.

For three days and three nights I prayed. So as not to break the welcomed stream of silence, I prayed with words only from my heart. It was as if God and I walked together up those mountain trails, hand in hand, in peace and long-awaited rest.

❦

"As a hart longs for flowing streams, so longs my soul for thee, O God," writes a psalmist with a seeking heart. "My soul thirsts for God, for the living God. When shall I come and behold the face of God?"[1]

Some years later, St. Augustine would phrase it another way: "For Thou hast made us for Thyself, and our heart can find no rest until it rests in Thee."[2]

Within each of us lives an empty space, a vacuum that nothing can fill except fellowship with the Father. God created our hearts to yearn for Him, to seek His face. In the quietness of our hearts, we ask, we seek, we knock, and God makes us a promise: "Ask and it will be given to you; seek and you will find; knock and the door will be opened to you. For everyone who asks receives; he who seeks finds; and to him who knocks the door will be opened."[3]

When we wait for Him, when we watch for Him, when we listen for His voice, we find Him. And, through the prayer of the seeking heart, we come to know Him, our Creator, the one who promises us rest.

Jesus and Elijah found Him on a mountaintop.

Mama found Him in a flower garden.

I found Him in an ancient monastery.

Have you found Him in your secret place?

God has already come to us. Now He waits for us to come to him.

How often I need to visit the mountaintop, to sit still and listen for the sound of fresh, cool spring water, water that will refill my empty pitcher and give me the zest and vigor I need to face another day. Even though Kappal, Switzerland, is separated from me by time and distance, I keep a bit of Kappal in my heart and travel there often.

ALONE WITH THE FATHER

Hot, thirsty, His feet still aching, Jesus finally finishes his all-day preaching marathon. Late that night, the crowds go home, their sponges full and dripping with the rich living water of God's word.

"Now," Jesus says to His disciples, "get into the boat and row to the other side of the lake. I'll join you later."

When the boat is out of sight, Jesus places one weary foot in front of the other and climbs up the side of the mountain.

Have you ever wondered what Jesus did when He reached His secret place of prayer?

Did He sing and dance and raise His hands to heaven?

Did He stretch out on the grass, feel the night's dew settle on His face, and talk out loud to the Father?

Did He sit on the mountain's edge and, in awe and wonder, gaze at the stars He had created?

Did He lie in the dirt face down and cry and agonize over those with leper's sores or blind eyes or crippled legs that He would not have time to touch and heal?

Did He, perhaps, see the vague image of a cross on some far horizon cast in uncanny light by the night's crescent moon?

We aren't told what He did. We are just told that He went alone into the mountains to pray.

I believe Jesus prayed in all these ways and many more. Perhaps Jesus climbed to the mountain's top, sat still, silent, and simply rested in His Father's arms. So very close to the Father, Jesus needed few words, if any, to communicate. Maybe they just sat there together, Father and Son, enjoying each other's presence, in quiet, restful fellowship. A prayer without words. A prayer from the heart.

And what happened when Jesus left His place of solitude and journeyed back into the routine business of living? Again, we aren't told, but please allow me to set the stage as it could have happened.

Jesus stands up, stretches, and takes a deep breath of cool mountain air. With God's voice still lingering in His heart, He walks slowly down the side of the mountain, refreshed, smiling. The late night breeze carries with it the bleat of a sheep, a young lamb that has wandered away from the rest of the flock.

In the moonlight, He sees one careless farmer's seeds, thrown on the mountain's roads and rocky ground.

At the bottom of the mountain, He steps with caution around a field of glorious wild flowers, being careful not to crush their velvet petals.

He leaves the mountain and walks toward the moonlit lake to meet His friends. But the night will offer Him no rest. Before morning comes, Jesus will have walked across the lake, rescued Peter from drowning, and calmed a mischievous wind.

"When they had crossed over, they landed at Gennesaret and anchored there. As soon as they got out of the boat, people recognized Jesus. They ran throughout that whole region and carried the sick on mats to wherever they heard He was."[4]

And once again, Jesus faced the demands of a busy workday, a workday that would, no doubt, last much longer than nine to five. But Jesus had new zest to His voice when He opened His mouth to speak. There was new vigor in His step. For He had been to the mountaintop. He had dipped his cup into the mountain stream, and His spirit had been refilled.

Remembering His trek down the mountain, the sheep, the seeds, the wild flowers, I can just hear Him now, preaching to the hot and sweaty crowds. . . .

"If a man has 100 sheep, but one of the sheep gets lost, he will leave the other 99 sheep on the hill. He will go to look for the lost lamb. . . ."[5]

"Listen! A farmer went out to sow his seed. As he was scattering the seed some fell along the path, and the birds came and ate it up. Some fell on rocky places, where it did not have much soil."[6]

"Stop worrying! Look at the flowers in the field. See how they grow. They don't work or make clothes for themselves. But I tell you that even Solomon with his riches was not dressed as beautifully as one of these flowers."[7]

DEEP PEACEFUL REST

The prayer of a seeking heart. I remember going shopping as a little girl one Saturday with my mother and Mama. After a full day of trying on clothes and comparing prices, I was exhausted. When Mom pulled into the last shop's parking lot, I asked if I could stay in the car. Mama offered to stay with me, and, in the quietness of the front seat, together we waited.

Mama and I had waited together many times before, but for some unknown reason the next few moments in the car became a memory snapshot I filed alongside some of the life-changing high points of my life.

My eyelids heavy, my limbs limp, I leaned my head over on Mama's shoulder. I can still hear her rhythmical breathing; I can still feel the soft wool of her coat against my face; I can still smell the familiar scent of lavender. Never have I been more aware of such deep peaceful rest.

Mom finished her errand and we drove home. The extraordinary once again became the ordinary. But I'll never forget that moment when we sat there together, grandmother and granddaughter, enjoying each other's presence, in quiet, restful fellowship. When my weary heart seeks rest, that's the kind of comfort I find with the Father. It's worth the long hike up the mountainside. Because there I come to know more intimately the One who loves me, the One I can trust, the One who has promised never to leave me.

❦

Our hearts seek the comforting shoulder of our loving Father. Yet, as we live in the hectic pace of everyday life, in the arena of the ordinary, it's easy to overlook the urgent needs of a yearning heart. Life is filled with distractions, distractions that shackle our eyes and ears and hands and minds. The heart begs for equal time, but its gentle voice can often not be heard above the swarming crowds.

This is why you and I need a secret place, a place of solitude, where we can find rest with the Father, where we can wait and watch and listen and prepare our hearts to hear His calming and reassuring voice. For God speaks to us in quiet ways, ways we might miss if we fail to retreat to the mountaintop faithfully. How easy it is to miss the extraordinary in the midst of the everyday ordinary.

LIVING IN THE ORDINARY

The ordinary in life is like figuring April 15th income tax—we don't like to do it, but it has to be done. It's much more exciting to experience the extraordinary.

What is the *ordinary*?

36

"Mommy, did you feed the guinea pigs?"

"Denise, did you mail the insurance forms, pick up the dry cleaning, and stop by the bank today?"

"Mom, will you help me with my live tarantula school project that's due tomorrow?"

"Mrs. George, haven't you finished that article yet?"

"Hey, lady, how'd ya say this sink got stopped up?"

The demands of the ordinary drain me quickly, and my thirsty heart needs living water. That's when I hear God's gentle call, a call more urgent than the clamor of the crowd. He beckons me to come, come to the mountaintop, far away from the madding crowd. "C'mon, Denise," He calls. "Let's find a quiet place to be alone and get some rest."

And without excuse, without guilt, I leave the dirty dishes in the sink, the checkbook unbalanced, and the family room floor unvacuumed, and I begin the long steep climb, step by step, up the mountainside.

Perhaps you, too, head often up the mountainside. There's no other place in the world like it. One of my favorite authors, Max Lucado, describes his nightly hike. In the late evening, as his family sleeps and the house is quiet, Max slips away to his secret place and listens for the gentle call.

"The quietness will slow my pulse, the silence will open my ears, and something sacred will happen," he writes. "The soft slap of sandaled feet will break the stillness, a pierced hand will extend a quiet invitation, and I will follow. . . . I leave behind the budgets, bills, and deadlines and walk the narrow trail up the mountain with Him . . . my sacred summit—a place of permanence in a world of transition."[8]

❦

Have you been to the mountaintop lately?

QUESTIONS FOR GROUP STUDY

1. What does this sentence mean to you? "He would have no qualms about leaving dirty dishes in the sink, the checkbook unbalanced, the family room floor unvacuumed. Prayer time with the Father was more important. It was the first item on His list of priorities."

– Why do you believe prayer was so important to Jesus?

– What does Jesus' prayer-retreat example say to us today?

– How important is it to give ourselves permission to rest in the Lord, to seek Him in the midst of a busy day?

– Is prayer time with the Lord the first item on your list of priorities? Do you think it should be, and why is it so vital to Christian living?

2. Describe your most recent personal prayer retreat.

– Was it significant?

– Were you able to relax from work and hectic schedules, and simply rest in prayer with the Lord?

– Did you feel pangs of guilt for taking time off? How did you deal with those feelings?

– When do you plan to take your next prayer retreat? (As a group, share prayer-retreat ideas and places.)

3. What does this statement made by St. Augustine say to you? "For Thou hast made us for Thyself, and our heart can find no rest until it rests in Thee."

– Do you find that statement true in your own life? In the lives of family and friends and people you know well? Describe.

4. What significant meanings do the image of the

mountaintop hold in Scripture? (For discussion, see Exodus 3:1-12, Numbers 33:38, Deuteronomy 34:1-8, I Kings 18:15-40, Matthew 5-7, Mark 5:11, and Luke 6:12.)

SUGGESTIONS FOR PERSONAL REFLECTION

– Plàn a prayer retreat. Arrange for a few days of uninterrupted solitude and plan to meet the Lord in a special place.

– Choose a place not too far away from your home so that your prayer time will not be used in long travel.

– If you invite a friend to go with you, discuss before you go how you will schedule your days. Help her to understand the purpose of the retreat and the time you will need to be alone.

– If going away from home, even for a short time, will not work out, plan a mini-retreat. Schedule several hours, or as much time as possible, and find a secret place where you can rest and pray without interruption.

3
...

Waiting for the Lord to Pass By

We don't know her name. We know only that she is a Jewish woman with an embarrassing medical problem. For the past twelve long and hurtful years she has bled continuously. She has spent all her money on doctors who promised sure cures for a hemorrhaging uterus. But her bleeding continues. Unchanged.

Money spent, energy drained, she is exhausted. Frustrated, sad, lonely, she has almost given up hope. She has stood on the mountaintop for years, praying with a weary heart, and wondering why the God of Abraham has not heard her cries for healing. She looks to her Father for relief, for a single ray of hope, for just one day without the loss of blood, yet she faces silence. Painful silence.

The disease that afflicts her is especially humiliating in

41

her society. Levitical law demands that no one touch her,
for the constant flow of blood makes her "unclean." The
law also prohibits her from touching anyone else, lest they
be made unclean.

She has been banned from the synagogue. She is no
longer welcome in the homes of her family and friends.
When she walks into town, Levitical law requires her to
shout, "Unclean! Unclean!" loud enough so that the town's
people can clear a wide path to let her pass. They want no
contact with her.

She yearns to keep her sensitive condition private, as any
woman would. Yet the Law dictates that she announce
publicly her affliction to family, friends, and strangers alike.

With downcast eyes, the women in the marketplace
grab children's hands and move quickly out of her reach.
Shopkeepers refuse her business and shoo her away lest
anyone dare handle a loaf or fish she has touched.

The dreadful disease of a dozen years sends scurrying
those she loves and those she so desperately wants to love.
She craves the warm touch of a friend's hand. She longs to
pat the head of a village youngster. She hungers to hug
once more her brother and sister. Late at night she dreams
of a husband's strong arms around her, and of little curly-
haired children asleep in their beds.

"Oh God," she cries out from the depths of her heart, a
heart so full of sorrow, so full of confusion, so alone, so
afraid. "Oh God of Abraham, please hear my cry. Please
hear my cry."

But the God of Abraham is silent.

A BROKEN PROMISE?

Her name is Sarah, and, to her deep distress, her men-
strual menses has ceased. Years before, her closest friends
came to her each month, always asking the same question:

"Sarah? Sarah?"

Sarah already knew what they would ask, and she appreciated their concern. But with each inquiry, her eyes would fill with tears as she sadly shook her head.

"I'm so sorry, Sarah, so sorry. But, Sarah, keep trusting God. Maybe ... maybe next month He will send *the* child," they would encourage her.

For years Sarah has waited and hoped and prayed for the child God promised to her and to her husband Abraham. But now her time has passed. Her childbearing years have come to an end. Full of sorrow, she gives the wooden cradle, the tiny handmade gown, and soft lamb's wool blanket to a young expectant friend. "I will no longer dream of becoming a mother," she whispers under her breath. "God hasn't heard my prayer. God did not keep His promise."

She feels she has disappointed Abraham, that she has failed him as a woman, as a wife. For several years he has seemed more and more withdrawn. She now spends her days slumped to her knees by the kitchen fire, crying in despair for the unborn children that will never be.

Infertility—the curse of the Hebrew woman in Sarah's time. Sarah is embarrassed by her barrenness. Yet, beyond her empty womb lies the most painful awareness of all. The God in whom her heart dwells will not answer her. And her world has become strangely silent. No hungry baby cries for her in the night. Her friends no longer ask her if. . . . And the One in whom she has placed her trust, her expectation, her life, is silent.

THE PROMISED MESSIAH?

Her name is Eve, and she has just discovered she is with child. Outside the gates of Eden, she gives quiet thanks to God, the One with whom she walked and talked.

43

She sadly recalls the deceiving serpent, her wrong choices, God's punishment to her and to Adam. They failed God. They disobeyed their Creator. They are judged guilty. They are banished from the Garden. They have known God's paradise, but now, in their time of despair and endless waiting, they are living and working in a paradise lost.

Eve places a calloused hand on her swollen middle and remembers God's warning to her deceiver:

"I will put enmity between you and the woman, and between your seed and her Seed; He shall bruise your head, and you shall bruise His heel."[1]

In intense shame, she didn't understand her Creator's words to the serpent. But now, after a time of repentance and reflection, God's words make perfect sense to her. "Her Seed." It would be by the woman that the Savior would come.[2] Redemption, restoration, reentry into Paradise would come through God's Chosen One . . . the One who would be born by a woman's seed.

"Yes," she smiles and looks up to the heavens. She, Eve, the mother of all life, would be the mother of the promised Messiah.

"After this time of God's silence," she tells her husband, "God now hears, God now speaks." And prayers of thanksgiving pour from her heart, a heart cut in two by the knife of rejection.

The pregnancy is difficult. After a long and painful delivery, Eve births a beautiful dark-haired boy and calls him Cain. And for the first time in a long time, she feels a bit of hope stir within her heavy heart. Then Eve gives birth to yet another boy. She names him Abel.

Eve watches her two sons grow and learn and become strong men. She notices how skillfully one tills the ground and the other tends the sheep. She observes with a mother's pride each son as he gives his finest fruit and his flock's first-born to God as an offering. In day-to-day anticipation, she watches closely for God's Messianic promise to be fulfilled. And each morning when she awakes from slumber, she looks toward the guarded gate and dreams a dream of paradise.

But one day, Eve's dream becomes a mother's worst nightmare. Jealousy erupts between brothers: Cain, her firstborn, slays Abel, her second.

And God is silent.

In one tragic afternoon, Eve loses both sons. And Eve loses all hope for freedom from sin's bondage.

DOES GOD HEAR YOU?

Are you suffering in pain and confusion, and no matter how long you pray, no matter how long you wait, you think God isn't listening?

Are you sinking into the quicksand of despair, your trust in God beginning to wane, for no matter how hard you pray, God never seems to answer?

Are you beginning to lose hope because your dreams have been dashed, and even though you pray sincerely, God seems far away?

I, too, have felt this way. I have sometimes felt like the man John Bunyan's Christian once met in his journey of faith, the man locked in the iron cage in the very dark room.

"Now, the man, to look on, seemed very sad," writes Bunyan. "He sat with his eyes looking down to the ground, his hands folded together, and he sighed as if he would break his heart.

"Then Christian said to the man, 'What art thou?' The man answered, 'I am what I was not once. . . . I was once a fair and flourishing professor. . . . I was once, as I thought,

45

fair for the Celestial City, and had even joy at the thoughts that I should get thither.'

" 'Well, but what art thou now?' asked Christian.

" 'I am now a man of despair, and am shut up in it, as in this iron cage. I cannot get out. Oh, now I cannot!' "[3]

The iron cage of despair. Have you been there? Are you now there, trying hard to wait, trust, and hope, but feeling discouraged and wondering where God is while you hurt?

Verna Birkey writes about this state of silent desperation, the "dark night of the soul." They are those painful hours, days, months, years, that no matter how hard we pray, God is silent.

"Nearly all the great saints of the past talk about 'the dark night of the soul,'" she writes, "when God seemed far removed and answers didn't come."[4]

Job experienced the dark night of the soul when, within a short span of time, he tragically lost his health, his children, and his wealth. Covered with oozing sores, he cried out in search of God: "Oh, that I knew where I might find Him. . . . Look, I go forward, but He is not there, and backward, but I cannot perceive Him. . . . I cannot behold Him; . . . I cannot see Him."[5]

David also prayed to God from his "very dark room": "To You I call, O Lord my Rock; do not turn a deaf ear to me. For, if You remain silent, I will be like those who have gone down to the pit. Hear my cry for mercy as I call to You for help."[6]

Jerusalem destroyed, the Temple burned, the Children of Israel captured as prisoners in Babylon, Jeremiah wailed from his own iron cage: "[God] has walled me in so I cannot escape; He has weighed me down with chains. Even when I call out or cry for help, He shuts out my prayer."[7] "Why do You always forget us? Why do You forsake us for so long?"[8]

46

The great prophet, Elijah, when pursued by the head-hunting, bloodthirsty Queen Jezebel, sank deep into the pit of hopelessness within the bowels of Beersheba's wilderness. " 'I have had enough, Lord!' " he said. " 'Take my life; I am no better than my ancestors.' " [9]

Even Jesus, Himself, dying on a Roman cross called out to His Father in agony: " 'My God, my God, why have You forsaken me?' " [10]

"Far worse than the breaking of [Jesus'] body is the shredding of His heart. His own countrymen clamored for His death. His own disciple planted the kiss of betrayal. His own friends ran for cover. And now His own father is beginning to turn His back on Him, leaving Him alone." [11]

Forsaken. Alone. Sinking rapidly into the realm of resignation. Crying out to God in torment and hearing only the inaudible beat of His own broken heart.

DARKNESS—THE TIME TO LISTEN

What should you and I do when our weary hearts cry out to God and He doesn't respond? What are we to do when we beg God to answer our prayers and we are met with unexplained silence?

Within God's word rests the secret. Within the lives of history's most faithful believers lives the answer. If we listen hard enough, we can hear God's gentle oft-unspoken whisper: "Dear Daughter, I have a reason for My silence. You are Mine, and because you are Mine, I can trust you with My silence. Wait. Be still . . . and know."

The secret? The answer? The heart's preparation to receive God's silence?

Faithfully waiting . . . quietly, prayerfully, attentively waiting . . . waiting for the Lord to pass by. Waiting . . . waiting with prayer-filled hearts and finely-tuned ears . . . waiting, listening, trusting, hoping. Sitting alone in the iron cage in a very dark room . . . knowing your Father is beside you and that you are never alone.

"Are you in the dark just now in your circumstances, or in your life with God?" asks Oswald Chambers. "Then remain quiet. . . . Darkness is the time to listen." [12]

When God was silent, Elijah simply, prayerfully, stood on the mountainside and watched, listened, and waited for God to reveal Himself. And God *did* reveal Himself to Elijah, in His own way, in His own time.

God also revealed Himself to David who, with great patience, endured God's silence: "I waited patiently for the Lord," he later wrote. "He turned to me and heard my cry. He lifted me out of the slimy pit . . . He set my feet upon a rock." [13]

Far from home, and made to wait in Babylonian chains, Jeremiah could one day shout with joy: "The Lord is good to those whose hope is in Him, to the one who seeks Him: it is good to wait *quietly* for the salvation of the Lord." [14]

It takes great faith to wait quietly, patiently, for the Lord. It takes great trust to know that God has a purpose in our waiting. And while we wait, we can be certain that God *does* hear the quiet prayers of our hearts. " 'Call upon Me and come and pray to Me, and I will listen to you,' " He promises. " 'You will seek Me and find Me, when you seek Me with all your heart!' " [15]

An attentive heart, a prayerful heart, is a searching heart. And the closer our hearts to God, the softer He needs speak to them. In the stillness of what seems to us a bottomless void, we can know that God hears.

"A wonderful thing about God's silence is that the contagion of His stillness gets into you and you become perfectly confident—'I know God has heard me.' His silence is the proof that He has." [16]

God has planted in our hearts the faith to know, and

even when our minds cannot understand Him, cannot comprehend Him, our hearts urge us to trust, to hope, to move onward through the fog of faith.

"Faith begins when I can no longer see, no longer understand. . . . I need the grace of endurance to forge ahead through the blackness. When I can see the outcome, that isn't faith." [17] So, we press forward steadily through the dark nights of our souls until God breaks the consuming silence and we hear His reassuring voice. And in God's seemingly timeless hush, while we seek Him with all our hearts, He reveals himself in ways unexpected, in ways pregnant with surprising promise.

"You will find that God has trusted you in the most intimate way possible, with an absolute silence, . . . because He saw that you could stand a bigger revelation." [18]

THE LORD PASSES BY

So, dear woman, whose hemorrhaging never ceases. Continue to wait, you who, for twelve years, are shunned by the religious society of your day, you who knows the disgrace of a disease that deems you socially unclean. Listen to your ancestor, David, when he tells you to "rest in the Lord and wait patiently for Him." [19] Wait, for in a short time, the Lord will pass by.

And when the Lord passes by you, don't be shy. Weave your way through the crowds, reach out and touch His robe, and let your long-suffering faith in God bring you healing. For the Lord will reward your faith in Him, and your healing will bring glory to the Father.

Then go . . . go and let the righteous rabbis examine you. Be full of joy when they loudly pronounce you "clean" again! Dance through the marketplace laughing, touching those you love, and patting village youngsters' heads. Dream your dreams for a husband and children.

49

And spend the rest of your life praising the One who hears and answers prayer.

❦

And you, Sarah, remain in God even though your child-bearing years are past. Even though you are living in the pit of despair, continue to trust Him, Sarah, even in your barrenness. For God is a God of miracles.

"[God] waits for us to despair of human strength and then intervenes with heavenly. God waits for us to give up and then—surprise!"[20]

Watch for His divine intervention, Sarah. And while you wait, retrieve the cradle, gown, and blanket! Stop crying; start knitting! You don't know it now, but God has a delightful surprise, nay, shock, nay, bombshell in store for you and Abraham.

Wait a few more years . . . until the eve of your second century of life. Then look to the stars and imagine their number. Run your fingers through the sea's sand and count the grains. For your unborn generations will out-number both.

And brace yourself, Sarah, for an angelic visitor. Be careful not to laugh when you receive the unbelievable news. If you must laugh, chuckle from joy, not from disbelief. For you, Sarah, will become a mother. A new mother! An *old* new mother!

When baby Isaac arrives, trumpet your announcements, doll him up, and show him to your friends. For his birth will show a nation, nay, a world, that God does, indeed, keep His promises.

❦

I've a message for you, too, Eve. Never give up hope. For even in His silence, God is a God of hope. God hears your prayers even as you pray outside the gates of Eden.

No, Eve, you will not be the mother who bears the promised Messiah. This is not in God's perfect plan. But one day, one day in God's time, a Jewish woman will birth the Savior. He will come just as God has promised. And through the seed of a woman, the seed of your daughter's daughter's daughter's daughter, He will redeem a fallen race. He will come to free all humankind from sin's bondage. And He will be called the Second Adam. With His own life, He will bring reconciliation to a prodigal world and reopen the gates of paradise.

QUESTIONS FOR GROUP STUDY

1. If you feel led to do so, ponder these questions as a group:

– "Are you suffering in pain and confusion, and no matter how long you pray, no matter how long you wait, you think God isn't listening?"

– "Are you sinking quickly into the quicksand of despair, your trust in God beginning to wane, and no matter how hard you pray, God never seems to answer?"

– "Are you beginning to lose hope because your dreams have been dashed, and even though you pray sincerely, God seems far away?"

2. *The iron cage of despair*—have you ever been there?

– Have you ever been trapped in a hard situation and thought there was no way out? What did you do? How did you progress through it?

– Was waiting in prayer, continuing in prayer, helpful to you?

– Have you ever felt so discouraged that you won-dered where God was while you hurt? Do you feel that way now?

3. What should you and I do when our weary hearts cry out to God and He doesn't respond? What are we to do when we beg God to answer our prayers and we are met with unexplained silence?
– How would you counsel a friend who came to you with these perplexing problems in her prayer life?

4. Do you agree that the answer to God's silence is "faithfully waiting . . . quietly, prayerfully, attentively waiting . . . waiting for the Lord to pass by. Waiting . . . waiting with a prayer-filled heart and finely-tuned ears . . . waiting, listening, trusting, hoping"?
– Why or why not?
– In what other ways can we deal with God's silence? List in order of importance.

5. " 'Call upon Me and come and pray to Me, and I will listen to you,' " He promises. " 'You will seek Me and find Me, when you seek Me with all your heart.' "
– What does this verse in Jeremiah 29:12-13 mean to you?

Ponder and Discuss.
6. Have you ever known the silence of God only to discover that He has entrusted to you a bigger revelation"? Describe the situation.

7. "[God] waits for us to despair of human strength and then intervenes with heavenly. God waits for us to give up and then—surprise!"

– Do you believe this comment? Why or why not?

– Describe situations in your own life, or in a friend's life, where this statement proved true.

SUGGESTIONS FOR PERSONAL REFLECTION

If prayer has become difficult for you, here are some suggestions:

– Reread the example of prayer given to us by Jesus, himself, in Matthew 6:9-13. Repeat the words of the prayer until you once again feel God's closeness and can once again pray the prayer without words.

– Simply rest in prayer. Find a quiet place and listen as the Lord speaks to your heart.

– In your quiet time, read some of your favorite verses of Scripture. Then close your eyes and contemplate the meaning of each. Allow God to speak to you through His Word.

– If you are experiencing your "dark night of the soul," seek the advice and help of a Christian counselor, pastor, family member, or friend with whom you can confide and share.

– Attend to the practical matters of life, such as: Are you getting enough sleep? Are you eating regularly and wisely? Do you take time out during your busy days to rest? Are you presently involved in hard situations that you find difficult to deal with? (Often, a better schedule, a less stressful day, and/or a timely visit to a medical doctor for a thorough physical examination can be helpful to your prayer life.)

Section II

The Listening Heart

(When we hear His gentle whisper,
we come to love God.)

Then a great and powerful wind
tore the mountains apart
and shattered the rocks before the Lord,
but the Lord was not in the wind.

After the wind there was an earthquake,
but the Lord was not in the earthquake.

After the earthquake came a fire,
but the Lord was not in the fire.

And after the fire came a gentle whisper.

(I Kings 19:11-12)

4

...

Listening for the Father's Voice

The gentle tap of summer's rain beckons me to stretch my nine-year-old frame upon the family-room floor and listen. I feel a cool August breeze blow my pig-tailed braids as it passes through the back porch screen door. The woodsy scent of summer drifts through the hickory nut trees, and renews my play-tired body, refreshes my childish spirit. The music played by the symphony of ten thousand raindrops upon the tin porch roof of my grandparents' farmhouse lullabies me into deep rest. Ten, twenty, thirty years will flow by, and much of my childhood will be forgotten. But the spectacular tap-tap-tap upon the tin roof will always induce in me a sense of restful serenity.

"'Nisey?" Mama calls softly and lightly strokes my tousled hair. "'Nisey? Wake up, 'Nisey."

I stretch long and lazy like an old calico cat, and then spring swiftly to my feet. It's *that* time of day, the hour I most await. Lunch!

Crispy fried chicken, Papa's Big Boy tomatoes, hot buttered corn on the cob! I can already smell cornbread baking, fresh okra frying in the cast iron skillet, and pound cake—rich and sweet—cooling on the wooden counter.

Mama's traditional southern lunch. I would hold onto the aroma that overflowed my grandmother's small farm kitchen long after the okra and tomatoes and corn ceased to grow in the backyard sunshine.

Lunch is over. My tummy is filled. The rain has stopped. Summer's sun has resurfaced. I am renewed. And, in no time, I am splashing through the puddles and running beneath the branches of the backyard shade trees, unaware that the happy days of childhood upon that little farm won't last forever.

Childhood. How beautiful it can be. How quickly it passes by. How short the season of spring and summer within the span of one's existence. For with the end of summer comes suitcases stuffed with memories and the long trip toward the advent of autumn.

🍎

I turned forty this year. It crept up on me like a tiger, then pounced and took me by surprise. I wasn't ready for it.

On my fortieth birthday, so longing for the disappearing little girl in me to tarry, I bought myself a pair of roller skates—hot pink roller skates. My friends laughed. They knew I hadn't skated in thirty years. But I skated anyway. For a little while. Then I went home, soaked my aching muscles in a tub of hot water, and took a nap. A long nap.

John Patrick in *The Teahouse of the August Moon* says that "pain makes men think." I say: "Forty makes women think!" How different life looks on this side of youth.

Forty years old. Yesterday I saw a photograph of my grandmother the year I was born. Gray hair. Rounding figure. Cotton print housedress. It dawned upon me that I am not much younger now than Mama was at my birth. Now she is gone, as is my grandfather. And the young green tomatoes he left on the vines on the morning of his death have ripened blood red and fallen away, never to grow again.

Now, almost a decade later, while the weeds overcome the once-bountiful gardens, I sit by a screen door on an August afternoon and dream of the symphony of a long-ago rain.

THE DEATH OF A CHILDHOOD

Have you ever paused and wondered: What is the use of life? The moment we are born, we begin to die. We live, we work, we hurt, we lose . . . we die. What *is* the use of life?

I feel drawn to deeper contemplation of this century-unchanging question when I most keenly feel the heartbrokenness of loss. Or when I feel the sadness of the years that frustrate my desire to spring to my feet with the nimbleness of a nine-year-old. Or when I miss those with whom I shared a piece of my heart, those whose most inward thoughts became my thoughts, those whose words and kindnesses I carry in the treasure chest of my soul.

Perhaps I ponder it most passionately when I realize how much, even now, I miss Mama and Papa, and the warm summer rain and the cool August breeze and the fresh okra frying in the cast iron skillet. For when they passed on, a part of me passed on with them. In some ways, Mama's and Papa's deaths signaled the death of my childhood.

And nobody calls me *'Nisey* any more.

❧

God's Gentle Whisper

Yesterday, at her request, I had lunch with a "forty-something-year-old" Christian woman I had not met before. She just wanted to talk, for she had a heart full of frustration.

As she began to pour out her story, I thought of the many other women who had recently relayed the same message to me. Basically, she was tired. The load of teen-rearing and housework had taken its toll on her body. She worked at a full-time job, a job that held little meaning, offered few dollars, and discouraged her God-given creative talents. Spiritually, by her own admission, she was empty, stale, depleted. She didn't hear the Father's voice anymore.

"The child in me enjoyed the parade of life, the surprises, the noises, the festive floats that flew so quickly by," she cried. "The adult that I am, however, sees the parade of life in a different light. It brings some joy, but the surprises hold no wonderment any more. The noise is often too loud and confusing, and the festivity is over before I am ever able to make much sense of it. While I try to contemplate the deeper meaning of the parade, a profusion of pandemonium passes by."

Her parade metaphor pictured precisely her problem. With every painful sentence, I heard the same unspoken plea:

What's the use of life? Of work? Of prayer? What is really important in this ongoing parade of life, a parade that will proceed with or without my presence?

Just what do you tell someone who is frustrated with life, finds prayer difficult, and no longer feels God's presence? What can she do—what can you and I do—when we hit a stalemate in our faith? How can we tune in and once again prepare our hearts to listen and hear the Father's voice?

DUST BOWL FAITH

Flat faith. I've been there, there in the pit of despair, so depressed, so discouraged, so far from feeling my Father's nearness. The faith that has lost its sparkle, its vitality, its expectation is not an uncommon encounter for women today.

Perhaps you are there now. Or perhaps you've been there in the past.

Faith residing in the great Dust Bowl. Perhaps you remember the Dust Bowl, or you've heard your parents or grandparents talk about it. More than 50 million green growing acres in the Great Plains region of southwestern United States turned to dust in the 1930s.

Why? Insufficient rain was one reason. But the primary cause was neglect of the soil. Before and during World War I, farmers planted large crops of wheat. But, in the process, they didn't consider the needs of the unsecured soil. The grown wheat couldn't protect the land during the frequent hot, dry periods. Eventually, after years of disregard, the rich dark earth turned to dust, and severe wind storms swept the earth right out from under the farmers' feet.

Neglected prayer time, disregarded Bible study, and lack of regular and meditative fellowship with the Father lead to a personal dust bowl of faith.

But there is hope. In Christ, there is always hope.

❦

You tell me you no longer hear God's whisper? You no longer feel His presence? You want to find faith's Fountain of Youth and dip yourself into its cool spring water and be bathed with spiritual renewal? You want to wash off the dust of discouragement and once again feel the living, breathing flesh of faith?

Come. Take my hand. Let us journey through the dust bowl together.

APPOINTMENT WITH THE LORD

First stop. You and I sit on a hillside covered with tender young pines. Except for the sound of a soft breeze, all is quiet. The world sleeps. We watch as the sky turns from midnight blue to rose to the golden shade of sunrise. The stars that peeked out through the dark blanket of sky only minutes before, disappear. We can see just a sketchy trace of a half moon. We do not speak; we listen, we listen to the sounds of silence. We sit still on the grassy hillside in the presence of God, the Creator of light and sunrises and moon and stars . . . and we delight in His goodness and generosity.

When we sit quietly with the Lord, waiting, watching, listening, we sit in the presence of a Friend. We need no words. For within us our hearts spill over with gratitude, with child-like wonderment.

In the quiet, you turn to me with a question. "How," you ask, "how can anyone sit on an early morning hillside and see the beauty of the universe and not believe in God?"

I don't have an answer. I, too, sit and wonder: "Oh Lord, for this lovely universe, to whom does the nonbeliever say, 'thank you'?"

Morning is the time for prayerful listening. Every morning, on appointment with the Lord, in a secret place.

Jesus loved the mornings.

"Early the next morning, Jesus woke and left the house while it was still dark. He went to a place to be alone and pray." [1]

After the death of her baby granddaughter, her namesake, and on the road to spiritual renewal, Catherine Marshall awaited each morning's sunrise.

"I am beginning to look forward to these early morning times," she writes. "There is an air of expectancy inside me as I watch the sun rise and wait for the Lord."[2]

She continues: "I'm beginning to understand why it is so important that I begin my recovery period early in the morning. . . . In the early morning we are freshest in body, mind, and spirit. There is the freshness of the day itself. It is quiet. Fewer distractions and voices to jam the wavelengths between us and the Lord."[3]

Meeting the Lord in the early mornings means starting our day in a wonderful way, and keeping the rich close fellowship with Him alive all during the day. One of my favorite people, author Warren Wiersbe, explains:

"I cannot emphasize too much the importance of daily quiet time with the Lord. . . . Meeting God in the morning means that you fellowship with Him all day long. At different times during the day, you will find the Holy Spirit speaking to you. Listen! There will be occasions when your heart will reach out for God. Pause and love Him! It is as you abide in Him all day long that He is able to work in and through you."[4]

So let us climb that grassy hillside, sit in our secret place early every morning, and meet the Lord there. Let us bask in the sunrise of His love for us, and thank Him for the privilege of His presence. For "the life of God given to [people] is the same life that energizes the entire cosmos. It sustains the universe. It is the essence of being. The best a mere mortal can do is to go quietly to some place, still, alone, there to meditate before the splendor of our God."[5]

THANKING GOD IN THE WAITING MOMENTS

Second stop. You and I climb into my little red car and we take off. Traffic jams. Long red lights. Backed up tunnels. Stalled cars halting cars.

(And we thank God for the few moments He gives us in our waiting to think about Him.)

In and out of the car all day. Buy milk at the grocery store. Pick up stamps at the post office. Fill our tank with gasoline at the station. Deposit a check at the bank. Wait in line at the dry cleaners.

Long lines. Everywhere. Waiting, advancing forward one step, moving back two steps. Just the average day of today's busy woman, wife, mother, grandmother.

(And we thank God for the few moments He gives us in our waiting to think about Him.)

For the Christian woman, long lines and stalled cars in the fast flow of life's traffic invite opportunities to meditate. In those precious minutes, we center our thoughts on God, and we wonder, we ponder, we remember, and our hearts take on the challenge of understanding God's grace. Constant communion with the Father keeps our spirits renewed, our faith refreshed. For God is only a thought away, a prayer away. Always. When God is in our hearts, He's never very far from our minds.

What is Christian meditation?

"Meditation is the activity of calling to mind, contemplating, thinking over, dwelling on, and applying to oneself, the various concepts that one knows about the promises, purposes, and ways of God," writes my friend, Ray Burwick.[6]

Christian meditation is a form of silent prayer, the prayer of the heart. While our bodies know the bondage of grocery store lines and traffic-jammed cars, our minds and hearts are free, free to roam unhindered throughout the heavens. Free to enjoy the presence of God. And, because of grace, God's amazing, unlimited grace, our minds and hearts can speak—uninhibited—to the Creator of the heavens.

While some see prayer as simply a religious exercise,

you and I can know that prayer is "the very breath and heartbeat of our lives." Prayer is "a friend sharing his heart with his Friend and growing in love and faith." [7]

LISTENING TO THE LORD
THROUGH SCRIPTURE

Third stop. Sit here silently with me and let us open God's Word. Scripture is the primary way we listen to the Father's voice. It is yet another way to pray.

"[God] speaks to us in His Word, and we speak to Him from our hearts." [8]

As you and I sit silently together and read the Scriptures, you hear an unusual shuffle of feet beside you.

"Denise?" you whisper. "Listen!"

Instinctively, at the same time, you and I turn around to look.

"Useless! Useless! Completely useless!" blurts out the stranger in royal blue garb. "All things are useless. What do people really gain from all the hard work they do here on earth? People live, and people die. But the earth continues forever."

The strange old man looks you and me directly in the eye. We are too stunned to speak.

"Everything is boring. . . . Words come again and again to our ears. But we never can hear enough. . . . There is nothing new here on earth." [9]

"Solomon?" You punch my arm and we both stare with mouths agape.

What an opportunity! We fire questions at him point blank as he pauses and considers his response to each inquiry. Then, across the miles of unmarked millenniums, he speaks his words of wisdom. You and I listen. Spellbound.

"Are you two living for the Lord or for the things of the world?" He sets his thick dark brow and asks us.

"Remember, I knew God and was greatly blessed by Him, yet I turned from the Lord and went my own way. No wonder I became pessimistic and skeptical as I looked at life! I didn't have God's perspective because I wasn't living for God's purposes. . . . Turn from the futility of sin and the world, and put your faith in Jesus Christ." [10]

Before we can catch our breath, we hear another voice.

"Do not love the world or the things in the world, you two," the voice forcefully interrupts. "If anyone loves the world, the love of the Father is not in him. These are the evil things in the world: wanting things to please our sinful selves, wanting the sinful things we see, being too proud of the things we have. . . ."

You punch me again and point. "John?" you ask. We are wide-eyed.

"None of those things comes from the Father," he continues. "All of them come from the world. The world is passing away. And everything that people want in the world is passing away. But the person who does what God wants lives forever." [11]

Solomon shouts out in hearty agreement.

"Life is filled with difficulties and perplexities and there's much that nobody can understand, let alone control. From the human point of view, it's all vanity and folly."

Then, for the first time, we see Solomon smile.

"But life is God's gift to us and He wants us to enjoy it and use it for His glory." [12]

Suddenly, in front of us, One steps forward and holds out His hands, One I have personally known since my ninth year:

"Dear children," He whispers. "I came to give life—life in all its fullness." [13]

The room is expectantly quiet. You and I hold the book

tenderly in our hands, the book that has answered life's most perplexing, most quizzical questions, for so many who asked, for so many many years.

In our quiet moment of reading the Scriptures, you and I join hands with Christians across the world, across the centuries. We read the same words of encouragement, the same messages of hope. We read God's Word as if the writers stand beside us, so close to us we hear their breathing, so near we feel their hands resting gently on ours. They share with us their dreams, their visions, their struggles, their revelations, their sorrows, their faith, their lives. And thousands of years later, through their Spirit-inspired words, they come alive to us again and again, and they offer us their most intimate, inward words of hope and love and promise.

"The Bible is God's message to everybody," writes Elisabeth Elliot. "We deceive ourselves if we claim to want to hear His voice but neglect the primary channel through which it comes. We must read His Word. . . . We must live it, which means rereading it throughout our lives." [14]

We read. And we listen. We listen to the voices that are only quieted when we refuse to hear. You and I hold within our hands, our hearts, living words . . . words that speak to us from the depths of mystery. Words that open blinded eyes to truth. Words that change lives. Words that offer life . . . now and beyond . . . life abundant and eternal. Life, given to us as a free gift, but a gift costly to the generous giver.

Each time you and I open its cover, we step into the pages and meet people of the past like ourselves, people who believe but are often weak, people who trust but sometimes worry, people who follow but unfortunately fall. We find ourselves on every page in those who hurt

67

and question and criticize, in those who drift in and out of the Father's fold, the Father's will.

"As we better understand what the Bible record says, we can better apply it to the needs of people today. This is the work of the imagination—building a bridge of truth from an ancient Book to needy hearts today." [15]

"Listen!" you lean over and tell me. "Do you hear them?"

I listen and I hear the music of a shepherd boy's harp in a far away field as he cares for his sheep and sings a child's praises to God.

I listen and I hear the words of shame and embarrassment pouring from the heart of a woman at a well at noonday as she offers a drink of water to a tired stranger.

I listen and I hear the sigh of contentment in Daniel's snore as he sleeps in an iron cage next to a ravenous lion that has been divinely reduced to a purring kitty.

I listen and I hear a stuttering Moses speaking to God before a burning bush.

I listen and I hear the rat squeaks in a dungeon, a very dark room that reeks with the stench of dampness, of death, and I watch a chained Paul scratch on parchment his love for a young church.

I listen. And I hear the words of mystery, the words of life and death, the words of life everlasting, the secrets of the universe.

> "Words and deeds of Christ our Master,
> Pointing to the life and way,
> Still appealing, still inspiring,
> 'Mid the struggles of today." [16]

CALLING TO THE CHILD WITHIN US

Our journey together ends. We go our separate ways, richer in faith from our shared experience with the Living Word.

But before we part, we open the book to one last word, and as we listen, we hear His tender call, His call that beckons us back to childhood. For God calls, not to the adult within us, but to the child.

"Come," He whispers. "Come to Me as a little child, watching with wonderment, waiting with expectation, listening with anticipation, following with innocence, trusting with sincerity, praying with unceasing simplicity."

He calls to the little girl within us, the child who marvels at the colors of the sunrise; the child who sees Solomon and David and Jesus come alive through Scripture; the child who yearns to strap on hot pink roller skates and take off.

When we listen to the Father's voice, we can hear Him calling back to life the child within you and me. The little girl isn't dead, she just sleeps. And just as Jesus "woke up" and raised the young daughter of Jairus, He can awaken the child within you and me to life again.

"God grant we may have the wonder of the child-heart that the Holy Spirit gives, and that He may keep our minds young and vigorous and unstagnant, never asleep, but always awake with child-eyed wonder at the next wonderful thing God will do." [17] I hear my Father's call, and years of adult-encrusted callus breaks loose from my heart. I am called back to my Father's simple, serene world of childhood. Free from worry, free from anxiety, free from guilt's bondage, free from the meaningless parade of pandemonium. I am given purpose.

And a life that was tired, frustrated, and spiritually depleted once again splashes in the puddles after an August rain and runs beneath the branches of the backyard's shade trees.

❧

With the voice of the Shepherd, and with the voices of the saints still speaking to my heart, I stretch long and lazy like an old cat. Morning . . . the time of day when my forty-year-old body claims yet another day of life, of age. Morning . . . the time of day when, through divine mystery, my childlike spirit is refreshed, renewed by a loving Father.

On this new morning, I listen to the gentle tap of summer's rain as it beckons me to rise. A golden-edge sun strains to peek over the horizon, as I lie in bed, snuggled between soft sheets, awaiting my daily awakening.

That's when I hear it, the familiar voice of the One I love, the One who calls me back to the freedom of childhood; the One who calls me to a life lived with purpose; the Shepherd who gave His life for this, His sleeping lamb.

Ever so gently I feel Him stroke my tousled hair, and I hear Him whisper to my listening heart: "'Nisey? 'Nisey? Wake up, 'Nisey."

QUESTIONS FOR GROUP STUDY

1. Ponder your childhood.

– Did you enjoy or regret your childhood? Are your memories good or bad?

– Did you receive genuine love from your primary caretakers?

– Did you receive spiritual nurture?

– Do you miss the years of your childhood, and, if so, why?

– What events in your childhood proved to be the most significant and why?

2. Have you ever paused and wondered: What is the use of life?

– Do you think this is a question asked frequently these days? If so, why?

3. Do you have a friend, family member, or acquaintance who is weary of life?

– What do you tell someone who is frustrated with life, finds prayer difficult, and no longer feels God's presence?

– How can you help this person through her spiritually-dry dilemma?

4. Do you agree or disagree with this statement: "Neglected prayer time, disregarded Bible study, and lack of regular and meditative fellowship with the Father leads to a personal dust bowl of faith"? Discuss.

5. Do you have a regular time each day to fellowship with the Father? If so, what time of day works best for you and why?

6. Throughout your busy days, do you frequently practice Christian meditation?

– What does Christian meditation mean to you?

– How has Christian meditation been helpful to keep your mind and heart prepared to pray?

7. Elisabeth Elliot writes: "The Bible is God's message to everybody. We deceive ourselves if we claim to want to hear His voice but neglect the primary channel through which it comes. We must read His Word."

– Do you agree with her statement?

– Why is the daily reading of, and reflection on, the Word of God essential to our lives as Christian women?

– What does the Bible mean personally to you? (If

71

time permits, allow each member of the group to tell what the Bible means to her.)

8. Reread the following Scripture passages that deal with the importance of God's Word. What are their meanings: Psalm 19:7-8, 119:105, 130; II Timothy 3:16-17; and Hebrews 4:12?

9. Warren Wiersbe writes: "As we better understand what the Bible record says, we can better apply it to the needs of people today."
    – Do you agree with his statement?
    – How can we "build a bridge of truth from an ancient Book to needy hearts today"? Is it possible?

SUGGESTIONS FOR PERSONAL REFLECTION

Set aside a special time each day to read a portion of Scripture, a time when you are at your freshest and best.
    – As you read, pause and ponder over those verses or words you don't fully understand.
    – Make notes of all that you want to study more fully.
    – Invest in a good Bible dictionary, and keep it close during your devotional times.

5
...

Earthquake, Wind, and Fire

In need of solitude and silence, and so wanting to be refreshed by uninterrupted communion with the God of creation, I retreat to the sea, the universal setting of serenity.

The rest I find at the shores of the sea has been a rare but refreshing step in my journey of life and faith, as "the waters turn the soul into a citadel of contented serenity with the spirit ensconced in quiet rest."[1]

I walk the ocean's edge and spread wide my arms toward its shore, waiting to receive a generous dose of divine rejuvenation. The child within bids me to kick off my shoes and run barefoot through the shell-strewn warm sand. From my pocket I pull a small loaf of bread, and within seconds, I hear the familiar flap of swift wings as seagulls encircle me, shrieking and swooping with silver wings to catch a crumb of crust. The sound of the sea surrounding me, the smell of salt air saturating my lungs, the treasure chest of blue water unfolding before me, my heart is drawn to prayer.

The hush of sea edge. Like a Beethoven sonata, the sea has a language of its own, a common tongue that touches those tired hearts that so seek the simplicity of solitude.

I close my eyes and listen to the gentle waves as they roll upon the shore. I feel an ocean breeze brush my hair, and sea mist kiss my cheek. I wait silently for the familiar sense of serenity to envelop me and wisk from my mind the hard work, hectic schedules, and everyday demands I journey to escape. I push far away from my thoughts the world's people and their problems, as I seek the sea's undisturbed tranquility and peace.

SOLITUDE AND STRUGGLE

But, to my dismay and disappointment, this day the sea offers no peace of mind and soul. I find no rest as I pause in his seaside presence.

For God has other plans.

I seek solitude, but I am met with struggle. Powerful, prayerful struggle. I yearn to pray the prayer of the waiting heart, the prayer in which I find such gentle peace. Yet I am compelled to pray the prayer of the struggling heart, the prayer of groans and sighs, the prayer of disturbing wordless passion for the world's lost and hurting.

The once welcoming sights and sounds of the sea instead become bitter reminders of a society that wrestles with weariness. The solitude with which I sought to massage my tired muscles, to uplift my listless heart, to renew my sagging soul, now opens the door to the faces, the cries, the perplexity of a planet's people. The sea's restful waters become instead restless waves. Instead of bringing consolation, solitude slaps my face like the salty sea spray. It demands that I open my eyes, my heart, my mind, and take detailed notice of a world that wrenches in pain.

I watch, I wait, I listen, and I am filled with anguish.

I hear the seagull's call, and it sounds like the voice of a small child who cries out in hunger and pain. . . .

I see a lone man walking the distant shore, and I ache with the grief of all those unknown to me who walk alone and lonely. . . .

I watch a mother and child stand silently by, as waves wash away their dream castle built on sand, and I hear the cries of the newly abandoned and the fatherless child. . . .

I stumble upon the lost limb of a starfish, and I sorrow for those who live with broken dreams and severed spirits, those I will never meet. . . .

And the solitude I seek far away from the clamor of the crowd becomes the solitude that brings me, oh, so close to them—compassionately close to the world's unknown others. I suffer with those people I will never meet, those strangers I cannot call by name in prayer.

And I learn compassion—the prayer of the heart, the heart of the prayer—the root, stem, and bloom of ministry through Christ to the world's others.

"Thus in and through solitude we do not move away from people," writes Henri Nouwen. "On the contrary, we move closer to them through compassionate ministry."[2]

I want to leave the ocean's edge, those dark turbulent waters that hold the vivid mental images of swollen bellies, pale faces, tear-stained cheeks, twisted limbs, and crushed hearts of a broken humanity. The massiveness of the sea makes me feel so small, so insignificant. I am reduced to one wee voice crying out to God for a fast-sinking society. The perpetual profusion of water holds within its immensity the breadth of our planet's perplexing problems. And I come to understand how weak I am in light of the work that needs to be done.

My hands reach out toward the sea, and, inside, I crave to hold the world's orphaned children, to build houses for society's homeless, to wipe the brows of Earth's battered, to hold the hands of those who have given up hope. But I am weak, so weak, so helpless to alone nurse the wounds of the world. I could more easily hold back the ocean's tide or breathe new life into an abandoned sand dollar than I could alone console Earth's sorrowing society.

I want to run away, far away into the sacred solitude that brings serenity, not suffering. But, alas, I cannot get my heart's consent. For my heart yearns to stay, to wait, to pray. So . . . I wait at sea edge. Patiently. I persevere in heartfelt prayer, and I beg God to move me, to convict me, to fill me with His compassion on behalf of a world of others. I pray the prayer of the struggling heart, and deep within I listen . . . I listen for the Father's voice in the midst of wind and sea and crashing waves.

CHARLOTTE'S WEB

I have a new friend who greets me every morning at my bedroom window. I call her Charlotte. All night long she spins and weaves and designs an elaborate web.

I watch with great amazement as she orders her small world, repairs a glistening strand or two, and waits for the dinner bell to ring.

This morning, Charlotte's web speaks to me in a unique way. I cannot carry the spider web analogy too far, however, or it will quickly tear apart. But I have noticed that Charlotte is well aware of what happens within her web. She is sensitive to, and instantly involved in, the least movement on any tender thread of her intricate home. For what happens within Charlotte's webbed world, what touches the lacework of her fragile facility, directly concerns and impacts Charlotte.

I believe the Christian's world is structured less like an orb and more like a web. When, through the prayer of the struggling heart, God grants within us the priceless gift of compassion, we can no longer live with others and stay uninvolved in their lives. Their hurts, their goals, their dreams become a vital part of our own hearts' prayers. For what happens within our wounded world, what touches the framework of our fragile habitat, directly concerns and impacts the believer in Christ.

Christ's compassion gives us new sensitivity. It commands, equips, and enables us to respond to others in His love, in His power. Through Him, we are challenged, we are empowered to reach out to a hurting world.

If only . . . if only we will listen for the Father's voice as He beckons us to prayer.

PRAYER OF THE STRUGGLING HEART

The prayer of the struggling heart. Does this prayer of our heart, this prayer too deep for words, touch the heart of God?

During His life on earth, Jesus showed us the Father's heart. For just as Jesus spread His arms and cried over spiritually-blind Jerusalem, I believe God cries over a lost humanity. Scripture affirms that God loves us, His human creation. Christ's weeping heart is but God's heart, a heart made not of stone but of life, living breathing life. If my selfish little heart can be so moved with sympathy for the world's suffering, how much more do His distressed children touch and move the Father's tender heart.

Do our persistent prayers ever change the heart and mind of God? Consider:

Elijah prayed to God seven times before he saw a small

cloud rise up over the sea, a cloud that would replenish the rivers with fresh water and end the deadly drought.[3]

Abraham prayed to God with nagging, annoying persistence on behalf of the people of Sodom and Gomorrah.

"Lord, what if I can find fifty good people? Will You still destroy the city?"

"Abraham, if I find fifty good people in the city of Sodom, I will save the whole city because of them."

"Well, Lord, what about forty-five?"

"Okay, Abraham, if I find forty-five good people I will not destroy the city."

"What about forty, Lord?"

"Okay, Abraham, forty."

"Thirty?"

"Okay, Abraham, thirty."

And on went the tete-a-tete between Abraham and God until finally. . . .

"What about ten good people, Lord?"

"You got it, Abraham! If I find ten good people there, I will not destroy the city!"[4]

When we pray, Jesus tells us to ask, to seek, to persist in prayer.

"Ask . . .; seek . . .; knock and the door will be opened to you."[5]

Does God respond to our prayers of struggle and sometimes choose to intervene?

Scripture answers this question. Consider:

Jesus touched blind eyes and made them see.

He healed lame legs and made them walk.

He called friend Lazarus from a grave, and gave him life.

The New Testament examples of God's intervention are too numerous to name.

And the Old Testament? Consider:

God parted the great Red Sea and led Moses to save His chosen children.

He sheltered a drowning Jonah within a fish's bowel.

He used a boy and a slingshot and slayed a Philistine giant. Yes, Denise, you say, but that's in the Bible. Does God intervene *these days* when a believer prays?

Please allow me to answer with a personal story.

We had been ministering in Boston's inner city, Chelsea, only a few years when street kids set fire to a large tire factory there.

It was an unusually windy day, and firefighters were unable to control the spreading flames. Without warning, the blaze frequently changed direction, turned back upon them, and consumed their city fire trucks. Volunteers scrambled to evacuate small children and the elderly from burning apartments. From our upstairs bedroom window, we watched the flames leap from house to house, until they reached the lawn of our home, and their sparks shot hot and loud at our window pane. I phoned my parents in Tennessee as we hurried to pack a few precious photos, an outfit of clothes, and an armful of treasured books.

Mom and Dad were leaving for their church's Wednesday night prayer service.

"Daddy," I called into the telephone. "The city is on fire. Our street is next to be evacuated. We're okay and will be leaving the city in a few minutes. So don't worry when you hear the news reports and can't reach us by phone."

Then the phone lines went dead.

Several minutes later, I looked at the clock. Eight-thirty. Just as we closed the front door behind us, to the whole city's surprise, the wind suddenly changed direction and died down completely. Weary firefighters fought the remaining flames and quickly forced them under control. Two-thirds of the city was saved from the devastation of fire. We didn't have to leave our home after all but slept that night in our own beds.

The next morning, Chelsea awoke to gray skies and air thick with ash. One-third of the city had burned to the ground. Fortunately, no one perished in the flames, and injuries were few. But I can still remember the eerie stillness, the people's shocked faces, and the muffled cries of the city's new homeless.

Two days later, telephone lines were reconnected, and I called my mother. I told her the whole story, the terror I had felt, the closeness of the flames to our home, the people crying in the streets, the city's shelters filling with families. I told her how the wind had suddenly changed direction, and how it had so unexpectantly died down.

"What time did the wind change direction?" she asked.

"Eight-thirty," I told her.

A long silence separated us. Then she spoke:

"That's the exact time our church prayed for you."

❦

Hebrews 4:16 tells us to come *boldly* to the throne of grace, that we may obtain mercy and find grace to help in time of need.

Yes, I believe the living Lord is hard at work today. I believe our prayers do touch His heart; I believe our prayers can change His heart and mind; and I believe our prayers will cause Him to sometimes intervene.

One thing's for sure. I am convinced that God, through a small church's Wednesday night prayer, changed the course of that Chelsea wind, one thousand miles away.

❦

But, it is not important that our prayers might somehow change the mind and heart of God. It *is* important, however, that we understand how much our prayers greatly change the mind and heart of the one who prays them.

When your heart, when my heart, retreats to a painful solitude and prays the prayer of struggle on behalf of an unknown other, we become different people.

"Solitude molds self-righteous people into gentle, caring, forgiving persons who are so deeply convinced of their own great sinfulness and so fully aware of God's even greater mercy that their life itself becomes ministry."[6]

When you and I enter into a dialogue of struggle with the living Lord, we discover anew who we are in this universal web. For when we pray for the brokenness of another, we also pray on behalf of our own brokenness. We, too, know broken hearts—believing hearts filled with Christ's eternal joy, but nonetheless hearts filled with human brokenness. For it is the brokenness of our hearts that lead us to Christ in the first place, the source of our salvation.

"How else but through a broken heart may Lord Christ enter in?" asked writer Oscar Wilde.[7]

How often does the pain of a broken heart drive us to our knees in confession, repentance, and in search of redeeming grace? It is there, in the iron cage of the very dark room of our soul, that we find God's gracious gift of forgiveness. It is there that God whispers to us: "Child, through my Son, Jesus Christ, I love you, I forgive you, and I give you the gift of life, abundant and forever."

We are all in the same boat in the immensity of Earth's sea, tossed to and fro by hard-hitting storms, blown off-course and asunder by hard-driving winds. Yet, when we hold out our arms in utter helplessness to the one who can calm the sea, storm, and wind, to the Creator of all the seas, of all the universe, God reaches down and rescues us from the turbulent dark waters. We reach up to Christ in clear understanding of our weakness, our vulnerability, our certain lostness, our inability to save ourselves, and we call to Him who will freely extend His arms of grace and pluck us from the tempestuous sea.

Does God save us because we are worthy? No. He saves us because He is Love. Salvation is a gift of grace, nothing we can work for, nothing we can merit, nothing we can ever deserve. Just grace. God-given loving grace.

When we pray with compassion on behalf of others, we enter into the suffering and compassion lived and taught by Christ, Himself. Through the prayer of the struggling heart, we discover anew our unique solidarity within the heart of humankind. As you and I seek solitude, the kind of solitude that solicits struggle, we hear the Father's voice as He calls us to the ministry of loving compassion.

THE PRAYER OF SELFLESS STRUGGLE

Elijah lived his entire life in loving compassionate ministry to others. He prayed the intense prayer of struggle as he persevered on the mountainside and listened patiently for the Father's voice. Elijah felt deep compassion for the Children of Israel. He grieved to see them live in sin and shortcoming, ignore Yahweh, and bow down and kiss the feet of the god, Baal.

More than 560 years before the birth of Christ, Elijah waited, Elijah struggled. No doubt, he wanted to turn and run away, but in his time of prayerful solitude, in his time of struggle, his heart would not be moved. He waited, he watched, and he listened. In expectation. In anticipation. He waited with a heart prepared to hear the Father's voice.

When you and I read Elijah's mountainside encounter, can we not somehow sense his dedication to the prayer of the struggling heart? Listen . . . can you not hear the turmoil, the fear, the strength of devotion in his voice?

"A great and terrible wind is roaring around me. Great

mountain boulders are breaking loose and crashing to the valley below. I am holding on tight in hopes that I, too, won't be blown away by this powerful wind."

["Elijah," we tell him: "Listen to the wind! Listen for the Lord to speak to you. Don't you remember that God once spoke to you in the wind, when the sky became black and clouds rose up over the sea, and rain showered the earth and ended the famine of your prophecy?"]

"Yes, I remember it. I am listening in the midst of the wind, but God does not speak. Wait! A great earthquake roars beneath me. The earth shakes and splits around me and threatens to capsize this great mountain. I fear I will be crushed by the earth's violent vibrations."

["Elijah, continue to listen while the earth quakes 'round you, for surely God will speak to you above the crash and clamor. He has often spoken to you in dramatic ways, ways steeped in majesty and mystery. Do you not remember the ravens that brought you bread and meat by the Brook Cherith, and the angels who fed you in the Beersheba wilderness? Do you not remember the dead boy God told you to bring back to life? Or the widow's handful of flour that became a bottomless bin? Drama, Elijah, drama and mystery . . . watch for God in the sensational, the spectacular."]

"I am listening. I am listening for God to shout to me above the noise and destruction, but God does not speak. God does not speak!

"But, wait. . . . Fire! Fire engulfs the mountain, the flames sweep around my head and feet. Surely, surely God will speak to me through the fire!"

["Yes, Elijah, God will surely speak to you through the fire, for you have said it yourself: 'God is the God that answers by fire.' Yes, Elijah! Listen, and remember when fire fell from heaven at Mount Carmel and consumed the sacrificed bull, and the wood and stones and dust, and even licked up the water from the trench. God spoke through the fire, and the prophets of Baal were destroyed, and the Children of Israel fell on their faces and cried out: 'The Lord, He is God! The Lord, He is God!'"][8]

"The fire burns hot and mighty, swallowing up the mountain. I am listening, yet I do not hear God in the smoke, the ash, or the fire."

With patience. With perseverence. With compassion, Elijah stands, waits, and prays the fervent prayer of selfless struggle. And all the while, he listens for the Father's voice.

❦

Patience. Perseverence. Compassion. The heartbeat of the believer's prayer. Surely, through these three, sandwiched within the sacredness of secret solitude, we become transformed to the likeness of Jesus Christ. And we no longer want to flee from the journey of prayerful suffering but, rather, to embrace those who suffer and wrap them in prayer.

Without a doubt, the prayer of struggle is the least worn path the praying heart chooses to travel, for it is lined with the sharp shells and splintered glass of a Christ-devoted life. But it is a path necessary for spiritual growth, painful as it is. For it is the path traveled by Jesus Christ, Himself, behind us, before us, beside us.

So, don't give up, Elijah! For just when we are about to give up the struggle of compassionate encounter, just when our prayerful patience and perseverence is severely tested by the earthquakes, winds, and fires of life. . .

God speaks to us in a gentle whisper.

QUESTIONS FOR GROUP STUDY

1. Have you ever sought solitude and rest in prayer only to be drawn into "the prayer of the struggling heart"? Describe.

2. Define the word *compassion*. Do you agree that compassion in prayer is "the root, stem, and bloom of ministry through Christ to the world's others"?

3. Henri Nouwen writes: "In and through solitude we do not move away from people, . . . we move closer to them through compassionate ministry." Do you agree? Why or why not?

4. Have you ever compared the Christian's world with the spider's web? What other analogies could you use to describe our link with a world in pain, with a world that needs Christ?

5. Discuss this statement: "The prayer of the struggling heart. Does this prayer of our heart, this prayer too deep for words, touch the heart of God"?

6. Ponder and discuss: "Do our persistent prayers ever change the heart and mind of God"?

7. Do you agree or disagree with this statement? "Does God respond to our prayers of struggle and sometimes choose to intervene"?
   – Have you ever had an experience where God directly intervened? If so, describe.

8. Reread Hebrews 4:16 and examine its meaning.

– What do you think the word *boldly* means in this particular context? (In the original Greek, *boldness* means "not keeping anything back," in other words, confessing everything to God.)

– Do you agree with this definition? If so, why is it so important to come to God *boldly* in our prayers?

9. How do our prayers prayed for the world's unknown others change our own hearts and minds?

– Have you been involved in situations where prayer for another changed you? Recount it, if group time allows.

10. Ponder the meaning of this question asked by Oscar Wilde: "How else but through a broken heart may Lord Christ enter in?"

– What does it say to you?

– Do you agree or disagree and why?

SUGGESTIONS FOR PERSONAL REFLECTION

Plan a certain time each day, either alone or with other believers, and pray for the needs of the world's people.

– Pray for the unborn babies, that they may develop strong and healthy.

– Pray for the mothers-to-be that they may be provided with nourishment and medical assistance to produce healthy children.

– Pray for the world's children, their spiritual upbringing, their diet, their home life, their families, their educations.

– Pray especially for the children who suffer from malnutrition and homelessness, for those orphaned and abandoned, for those handicapped, for those who will grow up but will never achieve their God-given potential.

– Pray for the world's families, for the world's leaders, for the world's elderly, for the world's sick and dying.

– Most of all, pray especially for all those without Jesus Christ, that they may know His love and receive Him into their hearts and lives.

Deeply ponder Hebrews 4:16 and the meaning of *boldness* in prayer. As a part of your daily devotional time, read slowly Psalm 139 and compare it with Hebrews 4:16 for greater understanding.

Reread I John 5:14-15. In the quietness of your heart, meditate on this verse and this question: Do you believe God hears our prayers?

6

...

God's Gentle Whisper

August 9, 1983. It is the last morning of her life. My beloved grandmother lies in a hospital 300 miles from my Kentucky home. Heavy with child, and so near my date of delivery, I grieve that I cannot be by her bedside.

Every day for a week, I have telephoned her, hoping to hear her gentle voice. Yet I am met with the same disheartening words: "Mama cannot speak. She's still in the coma."

I try one last time early this morning. My uncle answers the phone.

"I'm sorry, Denise, Mama cannot speak," he tells me. "She's still in the. . . ."

"Wait!" I interrupt. "Will you please just put the phone to her ear. I have something I must tell her."

He consents. And even though she will not hear me, I

yearn to tell her one more time how much I dearly love her.

"I love you, Mama," are the only words I say to her, for those are the words I want her to remember. Always.

I sit at the phone, and, for the next few seconds, I listen to the sounds of her deep quiet breathing. As I start to place the phone back within its cradle, I know I will forever wonder if she has heard my final words.

And then . . . then I hear a whisper, a faint wee whisper from the one I thought too ill to answer. I press the phone tightly to my ear, and strain to hear her voice.

And, to the amazement of all around, she speaks. She whispers, clear and sweet, six simple words that will echo within my ears throughout eternity . . .

"I know you love me, 'Nisey."

THE SAVIOR'S QUIET ARRIVAL

The year was around 3 B. C. A young virgin cradled within her tender arms her newborn child.

The Jewish world had awaited a Savior, a Deliverer from God who would save them from sin's bondage. They watched. They listened. They prayed. And they waited for the Promised One to come.

They anticipated a mighty king, adorned with jeweled crown and purple robes of royal resplendence. They expected Him to enter their world on a team of swift white horses, an army of five-star generals marching close behind Him. They envisioned their king victoriously slashing the wrist of the reigning Romans and forever residing upon Jerusalem's regal throne.

But God did not arrive armored with horse and army. He did not overthrow the governing heads of state. He did not set up His own great kingdom, headquartered in Jerusalem with His staff of majestic generals.

Instead, God came with a whisper. He arrived a baby,

tender and vulnerable, a child sustained and nourished by the warm milk of a peasant woman's breast. He came not by horse, but by donkey. He came not to throne, but to manger. He arrived surrounded by shepherds, not soldiers. Scraggly shepherds who stooped, soiled and smelly, before His infant feet.

God, in His own time, in His own unexpected way, parted the curtain of time and space, and stepped gently into human history, history that would never again be the same.

But human hearts were not prepared for His quiet arrival. Most of humanity missed God's coming as they gazed prayerfully toward heaven and awaited King Messiah.

THE GOD OF SURPRISES

God is the God of surprises. When we expect Him to shout, He whispers. When we expect Him to whisper, He shouts. Sometimes He answers our prayers in flashy foil-wrapped packages adorned with bright streamers and bows. And sometimes He wraps His answers in plain brown paper and dime store twine. We have no trouble hearing Him when He responds to our prayers with a trumpet's blast. But the gentle whispers? How easily we can miss them, overlook them, lest we press the phone tightly to our ear, lest we continually pray the prayer of the expectant heart, the heart always watching and listening for God's surprises. A heart prepared to receive Him.

How God must have enjoyed surprising Elijah! Elijah stood on the mountain and he truly expected to hear God's call behind the quake, His roar within the wind, His shout above the flame.

But God spoke to him with a whisper. An unexpected whisper. And only because Elijah had tuned his heart to the heart of God, and, with all his strength listened, did he hear God's soft answer.

91

God's Gentle Whisper

When Elijah was an old man, God had yet another surprise for him. He told Elijah to make one last journey. Young prophet, Elisha, walked with Elijah, and God lead them to Bethel, then to Jericho, and then to the Jordan River.

Perhaps while they walked, Elijah listened for God's whisper. Perhaps Elijah strained his ear in expectation of God's gentle calling: "Come home now, dear Elijah." Perhaps when Elijah's legs grew tired or when he faltered a step or two, he wondered when God would allow him to lie down and close his eyes in death's quiet slumber.

But just when Elijah expected to hear God's soft whisper calling him home . . .

SURPRISE, ELIJAH!

God sent from heaven a whirlwind of forceful fury, a chariot aglow with bright blazing fire, and a fleet of fast flaming horses to chauffeur Elijah into the arms of God!

What a way to go! (Can you just imagine the look of absolute astonishment on young Elisha's face?)

GOD'S WHISPER IN A HEARTBEAT

I awake early this morning, long before the first rays of new sun add rich color to my life. In the quiet shades of grayness, I lie in bed and count my rhythmic heartbeats. From the next room, I hear my children's breathing, their young hearts deep in restful sleep, their young minds heaped with hopes and dreams. And I ponder in prayerful silence the awesome miracle of life. The gift is life, God's gracious gift of breath and heartbeat. To my regret, for many years I have been largely unaware of this unique mystery, the remarkable miracle of a simple heartbeat, of a single breath of air.

Everyday mysteries, everyday miracles. Contained and carried within the ordinary hours of the everyday, the inconceivable becomes the commonplace, the utterly remarkable becomes the routine.

A baby is born . . . arms, legs, heart, lungs, intellect, talents . . . the mysterious conception in invisible seed, assembled and sustained within a woman's sacred nest . . . an awesome wondrous miracle so easily met with indifference amidst the humdrum of the daily mundane.

Prayer is like that, like the marvel of a heartbeat, the mystery of a breath, the miracle of a birth.

Imagine! Through prayer, you and I can call upon the One who fashioned our delicate bodies, who gifted our hearts and minds. The One who created us and gave us breath! The One who listens to us, our prayers of thanks and our prayers of complaints. The One who loves us so deeply that He would rather die than live without us.[1]

Imagine! Through prayer you and I can tune our hearts to the heart of God, our Father, ever-powerful and ever-present. We can commune with Him Spirit to spirit, thought to thought, privately, personally, as our hearts intermesh in mystery and miracle. Deep calling unto deep.

Oh, that you and I will never gaze prayerfully toward heaven with hearts unprepared and miss the wonder of King Messiah's coming. Prayer is too priceless a gift to squander, to misuse. The prayer of the heart is too precious to be packed with anything less than genuine awe.

Perhaps, just perhaps, God answers us in surprising ways to keep us listening in hearty anticipation, to keep us praying the prayer of the expectant heart, to keep us perched high up on our spiritual tiptoes in delightful expectation.

☙

Around 30-33 A. D. (A possible scenario:)

Jesus is arrested, betrayed by His own chosen disciple. Peter, sword in hand, stands ready to do battle. "This is it!" Peter mutters under his heated breath. "Jesus is now ready to wage war, to establish His kingdom."

The arresting soldiers grab Jesus. Peter pulls out a sword and slices off the ear of the High Priest's servant.

The battle has begun. Perhaps Peter expects to slice many ears, many throats, before the long night is over. He waits for the battle cry to come from Jesus' lips. Yet, no battle cry comes forth. Jesus, instead, answers Peter with a silent shake of the head, and replaces the servant's severed ear.

The disciples expect the shout of combat. With Jesus as their Commander, they anticipate winning the war, undefeated. Yet, as they see it with human eyes, the answer to their anticipation, the reply to their three years of expectant following and waiting is defeat. Jesus' defeat. Their defeat. In fear, they run away. Hiding, crying, denying.

GOD'S FORGIVENESS IN A WHISPER

Three crosses shade a mountaintop, a mountain shaped like a human skull. Jesus Christ hangs by spiked hands and feet between two seasoned thieves. A crown of sharp thorns cuts deep and encircles His bleeding brow. He says little; His agony is great. Above Him mocks a handmade sign: "Jesus, King of the Jews."

Quietly, head bowed in final prayer, Jesus endures the wrath of all hell's jeers and nears the great enemy, Death.

For the executioner, it's all in a day's work. He hits playfully at a co-worker.

"Hey, buddy! The one in the middle's just about gone. Should be dead any minute now. Your turn to unspike the body. I'm gonna hit the road. See you guys on Sunday."

The ultimate in indifference is seen at the cross of Christ. If only they knew that the Creator, Himself, had just given His life, His blood, His last breath, for His wayward creation.

If only they knew that God, Himself, had become a man, arms and legs, heart and lungs, intellect and talents—a man who, for our sake, had chosen to taste life as we live it, laughter and tears, joy and sorrows, birth and death.

But before He dies, He whispers sweet words that will echo in our ears throughout eternity. "Father, forgive them," [2] and "It is finished." [3]

The head honcho makes plans to go home, plop down in a La-Z-Boy recliner, put away a few lite beers, and flip on the Friday Night Movie. He expects Jesus to die like all the others. No big deal. Three more to crucify day after tomorrow.

But God refuses to allow his Son to die quietly. Messiah's death does not whisper. Messiah's death shouts.

The very universe responds to their disgusting indifference to God's Son with screams of retribution as the sun, moon, and stars hide their faces and cover the earth with an intense blanket of unexplained darkness. Beneath the foreboding blanket, the earth quakes, rocks break apart, and long-time graves are disturbed and opened.

The death of our Lord is announced with a shout. On the third day of His death, something happens. Something mysterious; something miraculous; something that will cause humankind to marvel for the next 2000 years and beyond. Jesus Christ stands up alive and leaves His place of burial. He arises from the tight fist of death.

Enter trumpets! Enter angel chorus lines! Enter cymbals! Enter reporters from the New York Times, CBS News, and Night Line. Sunday morning's headlines in all the major papers read:

"Christ Has Risen from the Dead!"

"Christ, Victorious Over Grave!"

"King of Jews Defeats Evil One!"

Hardly.

95

God's Gentle Whisper

His resurrection, the single one act of history that guarantees our divine destiny, that determines life and death itself, was announced with a whisper. To a couple of women and a group of disbelieving, bemoaning disciples.

Truly, God is the God of surprises!

❦

Through God's gentle whispers—His Christmas Whisper, His Whisper on Easter morn—God speaks to us His eternal words of love, of grace, of freedom from sin's bondage.

"I love you, dear child," He whispers to you and me, for those are the words He wants us to remember. Always.

As we look at our Lord Jesus, as we witness His willingness to suffer human life and human death, to carry our cross for us to the Place of the Skull, we can answer Him with six simple words of absolute certainty: "I know you love me, Lord."

QUESTIONS FOR GROUP STUDY

1. Name six ways we can prepare our hearts to hear God's gentle whispers?

   – How can we prepare our hearts to live in expectation and wonderment?

2. Why is God the "God of surprises"?

   – Have you enjoyed God's surprises in your own life?

   – Share some of the more delightful times God has surprised you.

3. Do you ever ponder the miracle of birth, of growth, of sunrise, of a flower's bloom, of a single breath of air, of

a healthy heartbeat?

    – Consider ways we can begin to take more apprecia-
tive notice of these everyday miracles in our lives.

    – Consider ways we can instill a sense of grateful-
ness for God's creation and goodness in the lives of our
children.

    4. Why is prayer like "the marvel of a heartbeat, the
mystery of a breath, the miracle of a birth"?

    – Describe what prayer means personally to you.

SUGGESTIONS FOR PERSONAL REFLECTION

    Discover ways that you can prepare your heart to see
and enjoy God's surprises.

    – Be aware of small things in life, such as a spider
spinning a web or a wild flower in your back yard, for God
can speak to your heart through all things, big and small.

    – Pay special attention to the events that envelop your
life. Is God speaking to you through one of these events?

    – Take time to sit quietly and listen for His still, small
voice. Take time to enjoy His creation of nature, of chang-
ing seasons, of children, of elderly people. Pay close
attention to the words they say to you.

    – Ponder those times you have distinctively felt God
speaking to you in a surprising way.

Section III
The Responsive Heart

(When to His whisper our listening heart responds,
we prepare to serve God.)

"When Elijah heard it,
he pulled his cloak over his face
and went out and stood at the mouth of the cave"
(1 Kings 19:13).

7
...

Standing at the Mouth of the Cave

Lucy reaches for the doorknob of the large old wardrobe. She expects it to be locked, but, to her surprise, the knob turns. She opens the heavy door and, like any other ordinary child of curiosity, she peers inside. Stepping bravely, but slowly, into the mysterious darkness, sweet scents of cedar tease her nose and old moth balls crunch beneath her feet.

Outside the wardrobe play Peter, Edmund, and Susan. Downstairs in the library, the owner of the great English manse, an old English professor with "shaggy white hair," studies yet another thick volume.

Inside the closet Lucy lingers, walking ever so slowly and searching in vain for the wardrobe's back wall. But, alas! The wardrobe has no end. As she passes cautiously through, she meets unexpected rays of sunlight and the soft touch of snow upon her small young face.

Lucy soon discovers she has entered a new world, a world invisible and unknown to adults, a world full of mystery, wonder, and expectation, a world far away from the old professor's English manse.

Lucy has entered Narnia!

Narnia soon becomes Lucy's favorite secret place, a place where she finds rare surprises and delightful adventures, a world far more fascinating, far more beautiful, far more remarkable than the visible world in which she lives. How she wants to stay there, never again to leave!

Lucy's extended visits to Narnia change her as it introduces her to a world she didn't know existed, a world she can no longer live without. Time controls no part of Narnia, for there time stands still. What seems hours spent in Narnia's time, prove only minutes in Earth's time.

With Narnia deeply embedded in her heart and mind, Lucy goes about her ordinary days of school and work, but Narnia is never far away from her thoughts.

Eventually, Lucy introduces Peter, Edmund, and Susan to the delights of Narnia. Separately and together, the children visit Narnia many times throughout their childhood. But no matter how often they frequent it, Narnia never loses its mysterious enchantment, and the children never lose their love for this, their new-found world.

And the old professor—the old white-haired professor? Well, he knew much more than he professed to know, for he always met the children (when they returned from their Narnian adventures) with a smile on his lips and a twinkle in his eye.

GOD'S WONDROUS WORLD

Of course, Narnia is an imaginary land that comes directly from the incredibly creative mind of C. S. Lewis as he captures the children's exciting adventures in his books, *The Chronicles of Narnia.*[1]

Nonetheless, I am finding much remarkable resemblance between the large old wardrobe that opened to Lucy the wondrous world of Narnia, and my own private prayer-closet that opens to me the wondrous world of God.

For instance . . .

The door to my prayer-closet is never locked but opens easily. And when I step into its majestic mystery, I find my Father waiting there to welcome me. My prayer-closet has become my favorite place to go, to tarry, a place far more fascinating, far more beautiful, and far more remarkable than the visible world I know.

Perhaps the visible world that seems so real is not the real world at all but a sort of "shadow-world," a shadow of the real world. Perhaps it is this invisible world, where we meet God in quiet privacy, where you and I as believers in Christ will spend all eternity . . . perhaps this world we cannot see is truly the "real world."

Like Lucy, when I visit my invisible world, I come back changed, I come back renewed, refreshed, rewarded with a heart more anchored in love in God's own heart.

Before I met Christ, I never knew this world of prayer existed. Now, many years later, God's open wardrobe has become my favorite passageway to a world I can no longer live without. And no matter how busy my day, no matter how hectic my schedule, my precious prayer-closet times are so deeply embedded in my heart and mind, that the Lord is never far away. It is the prepared heart that holds onto God's presence between the times of quiet solitude, between prayer-closet times.

How often I go into the Narnia of prayer with my hands empty. But I always come out with my hands full, full of God's joy and rich blessings. How often I go in with my brief case full, full of heartaches and headaches, worries and fears. But I find I can leave my brief case there, and come back relieved of the load with which I struggled.

When I step into my prayer-closet, I leave Earth's restrictive clock, and I move most willingly into God's time. In His mysterious presence, time seems to stand still. No matter how many times I visit the delightful world of my Father, the prayer-closet never loses its mystery and wonder and awe. And I never lose my love for this, my new-found world.

For inside those closet doors, those doors that open to me such perfect fellowship with my Father, I celebrate!

I celebrate Jesus Christ and the remarkable gift of his love for me, of His life to me.

I celebrate the beauty around me, beauty created for me to enjoy by the loving Creator, Himself.

I celebrate life, with its amazing heartbeat and breath, with its wondrous miracle of birth and bountiful new life.

I celebrate the little girl within me who wakes up in the mornings with "a prayer on her lips and a song in her heart," as my grandfather used to say. I am the child who still enters the prayer-closet with wide-eyed curiosity and wonder and expectation of surprise.

And I celebrate this priceless, precious gift of prayer, the honor of entering into the King's Royal Chambers as His beloved daughter, a member of His family.

Truly, prayer is a welcome haven from the turmoil all around me.

Oh, that I can introduce the prayer-closet to the Peters and Edmunds and Susans of this world! Oh, that I may personally bring them to the One who holds the mysteries of the universe in the palm of His hand, a hand plenteous with power, a hand laden with love . . . for you, for me, for them, forever.

THE PRAYER OF THE PREPARED HEART

I love my prayer-closet times, those times I can concentrate without interruption on God's goodness and generosity.

"We have to know someone before we can truly love them," writes Brother Lawrence. "In order to know God, we must think about Him often. And once we get to know Him, we will think about Him even more often, because where our treasure is, there also is our heart."[2]

To know Him better, to love Him more, I delight to sit in His tender presence and ponder the mysteries of faith and life. I love to open the book, His word, and run my fingers over the life-giving words, words that centuries of Christians have read and treasured. I could pitch my tent in Narnia and live there forever, enjoying and reveling in the invisible world where I and my Father are one.

But, bills must be paid, children fed, letters faxed, laundry washed, bathrooms scrubbed, kids car pooled, life's various matters attended to. From within the walls of my quiet solitude, I hear the impatient whine of a 27-cubic-foot refrigerator that waits to be refilled. Reluctantly, I leave the precious silence and reenter the chaos of Shadow-World. Once again I must step into the loud merry-go-round society that runs in meaningless circles like plaster-of-Paris horses with wide painted smiles and glazed glass eyes.

But I enter Shadow-World with a heart that never ceases to pray the prayer of the prepared heart, a heart that prays in spite of the chaos enclosing it.

I am learning that "ceaseless interior prayer is a continual yearning of the human spirit towards God."[3]

Above the noise and endless chaos, my human spirit strains to listen, to hear the gentle voice that calls me "come," a voice so easily drowned out by the incessant roar of Shadow-World, a voice that only a prayer-prepared heart can hear.

🍂

Shadow-World, with its duties and responsibilities, is somewhat like the valley that lies between the mountaintop experiences of prayer.

Some years ago, when my husband and I worked and attended school in Cambridge, Massachusetts, we occasionally climbed into our old '69 faded green Plymouth and drove through the mountains of Vermont.

Reveling about our break from books and typewriters, we stopped often, unpacked lunch and snacks, and sat on the quiet mountaintops to eat. Long after the peanut butter sandwiches disappeared, Timothy and I sat still and gazed silently out over the rows of rolling green hills, each hill with its own valley, each valley with its own village, each village with its own newly painted white church steeple.

Deep passionate prayer poured forth freely from my heart during those rare outings, those quiet hours of husband-and-wife solitude when Vermont's warm sunshine and gentle white clouds revealed beauty immeasurable and unspeakable.

But the dictates of time and the everyday demands of life told us we couldn't stay in quiet solitude upon a distant Vermont mountaintop. We had to come back to the world of dirty streets, tuition bills, broken water pipes, and unreasonable deadlines . . . the world where prayer can so easily be crowded out by the long lists of that day's "to do's."

Even Jesus, Himself, had to come down from the mountaintop, refasten His sandals, roll up His sleeves, and continue the work God gave Him to do.

106

PRAY WITHOUT CEASING?

How easily we can be drawn to prayer atop a Vermont mountain or within the enveloping solitude of our secret place. But how difficult prayer can be during the ticket-paying, toilet-cleaning, timecard-punching "meantimes" of life, those times when we must step out of God's time and back into Earth's demanding schedule.

I believe prayer is vital to our lives as Christian women. I heartily agree with Martin Luther: "To be a Christian without prayer is no more possible than to be alive without breathing."[4] The Apostle Paul urges us to "pray without ceasing."[5] Jesus tells His hard-working disciples to "come with me by yourselves to a quiet place and get some rest."[6]

If prayer is as important to our spiritual lives as breathing is to our physical lives . . .

If Paul asks us to remain in prayer continually, never ceasing . . .

If Jesus wants His followers to find a quiet place of solitude and rest in prayer . . .

If, if, if, for the twentieth-century Christian woman, then becomes how, how, how?

How can we spend a lifetime in prayer and fellowship with our Father when we have so much to do, so many places to go, so many needs to fulfill?

How can you and I, like Elijah, stand patiently outside "the mouth of the cave" and listen for God's gentle calling in the midst of earthquake, wind, and fire confusion that constantly distract us?

How can we so tune our hearts to the heart of God, that even when we are encircled by society's chaos, our hearts are prepared to feel His presence and hear His voice?

Even during—especially during—those times when . . .

107

We fill our trash cans full of garbage and the truck doesn't run . . .

We mail our bills, due yesterday, and the carrier doesn't pass . . .

Our teenager runs out the back toward the family car, while our toddler runs out the front, diaperless . . .

The simmering stew has firmly attached itself to the bottom of the pot, and dinner guests are ringing the bell.

In 1710 Matthew Henry wrote: "A gold thread of heart-prayer must run through the web of the whole Christian life."[7]

How can you and I weave any kind of purposeful, passionate prayer within and throughout the ordinary hours of our busy everydays? Pray as we breathe? Pray without ceasing? Escape to the mountaintop to pray in the middle of the day?

Impossible?

❧

We are women governed by time, husbands, homes, children, aging parents, office bosses, unbalanced check-books, and life-health-medical-house-car-dental-burial insurance payments.

Most Christian women I know rise early in the morn-ing, hit the floor running, keep an Olympic track pace throughout the day, and don't stop running, hauling, com-muting, chauffeuring, delivering, car pooling, and helping until late that night. In fact, I believe that if the Proverbs 31 woman were expected to carry the work and family load the average woman of today manages, she would throw up her hands and go back to bed.

Christian women today are deeply involved in the nur-ture of their families, in the maintenance of homes, in the work places, in their churches, in their neighborhoods and communities.

As believers in Christ, we want to reach out to those who hurt and grieve, to those who are hungry and cold, to the unchurched, to the lost, to the troubled. Yet, we are limited, so limited by dwindling time and energy in light of all that desperately needs to be done.

Pray without ceasing? Can it be done? How different our everydays would be if we could keep our hearts forever focused upon God, always listening, always prepared and ready to respond to His divine instructions.

THE PRIORITY OF PRAYER

Jesus made prayer and fellowship with the Father the priority in His life. Whether He hammered a nail into a board, reached out to heal a man born blind, lifted small children upon His lap, or took a whip to the Temple moneychangers, He knew that God was only a heart's whisper away. The Father and Son had unbroken communion throughout the days of Jesus' life on Earth. Jesus kept his heart focused on His Father while He worked, while He traveled, while He ministered.

"Christ used to spend nights in prayer (Luke 6:12). He often rose a great while before day in order to have unbroken communion with His Father (Mark 1:35). The great crises of His life and ministry were preceded by special prayer (e.g., Luke 5:16), 'He Himself would often slip away to the wilderness and pray,' a statement that indicated a regular habit. Both by word and example He impressed upon His disciples the importance of solitude in prayer (Mark 6:46, Luke 9:28)."[8]

I watched my grandmother follow Jesus' example of prayer, committing her time and energy to God, and praying that He would reveal His will to her concerning how she spent her hours. Mama began each day with prayer, ended each day with prayer, and wove the golden thread of prayer within and throughout all the hours of her day. In her work, in her walk, in her relationships with others, in her grief, and in her pain, the radiance of Christ shone from within her heart onto her precious face.

Mama discovered early in life the secret of unceasing communion. For she discovered that God is not only above us, below us, around us, and beside us. God, the Holy Spirit, lives within us. He is as close as our heartbeats, as near as our breathing. Our bodies are His temple, the place in which He resides. We might not always be aware of His presence, but we are never without His presence. So caught up in this merry-go-round life, we can sometimes forget the closeness of God. But Christ lives in the chapel of our hearts, a sort of "portable prayer-closet" we take with us, a secret place of prayer that's only a thought away.

Mama never sat upon a Vermont mountaintop to pray, but she prayed continually within the sanctuary of her heart. In the quietness of her soul, she lived on the mountaintop, in unending communion with God. Within the chapel of her heart, she came to know God, to love God, and to serve God.

Can't you tell the people who live on the mountaintop, those who dwell in conversation with God within the chapel of their hearts?

"Oh, their problems aren't any different. And their challenges are just as severe. But there is a stubborn peace that enshrines them. . . . A serenity that softens the corners of their lips. A contagious delight sparkling in their eyes. And in their hearts reigns a fortress-like confidence that the valley can be endured, even enjoyed, because the mountain is only a decision away."[9]

ALL THINGS BECOME PRAYER

Surely, as the gold thread of prayer weaves itself in and out and throughout our ordinary hours, God's presence enriches us through those prayerful pauses and puts meaning into the most mundane duties of our days. Even though we cannot see it now, those strands of shining gold are becoming a splendid work of art, weaving our everyday hours into the rich tapestry of a lifetime devoted to God. And God's loving fingerprints are braided deep within the tapestry of our lives, adding delicate design and delight to our everydays.

"To realize the intimacy of the Master's touch upon all the minutiae of my affairs, to experience His hand guiding, leading, directing in every detail of each day, is to enter a delight words cannot describe." [10]

When we put our hands in our Father's hand as we go about our hours, whatever we think, whatever we do, whatever we say, will be a form of prayer for us, and ministry for others.

The morning walk with a child through spring's first tiny wildflowers . . .

The beautifully-resolved conflict with our co-worker . . .

The homemade bread given to our elderly neighbor . . .

The ear we kindly lend to a nonstop talker . . .

The money we place in our church offering envelope . . .

The little scraped knees we bandage and kiss . . .

The courtesy we show a driver in non-moving traffic . . .

The kind words we speak to a rude waitress . . .

The way in which we gratefully view the evening sunset . . .

The way we invite God to direct our thoughts . . . thoughts true and noble and right, pure, admirable and excellent and lovely, praiseworthy. . . . [11]

111

When all things abide in Christ, all things become prayer, all things become opportunities for ministry, and the touch of Christ is upon each hour of our days, blessing it, enriching it.

Our hearts will know a strange, but beautiful, kind of peace, for the heart at peace is the heart prepared that practices the continual presence of Jesus Christ throughout the most ordinary days.

THE GOD OF THE SECOND CHANCE

The chapel of our hearts also provides opportunity for regular confession of wrongdoing. God extends His gift of forgiveness to us when we admit our wrongs and turn away from them.

God forgives us when, during the course of our everyday, we stumble and fall, when we make mistakes in relationships, when we pursue those thoughts and those things unworthy of God's presence within us. He allows us to get back up on our feet and start over again.

J. Oswald Sanders, in his book, *Spiritual Leadership*, puts this concept of forgiveness in a poignant way:

"A study of Bible characters reveals that most of those who made history . . . failed at some point, and some of them drastically, but [they] refused to continue lying in the dust. Their very failure and repentance secured to them a more ample conception of the grace of God. They learned to know Him as the God of the second chance to His children who had failed Him—and the third chance, too." [12]

Many times God has picked me up when I stumbled, brushed off my dusty clothes, kissed my forehead, and, through His gift of grace, given me a second chance. And a third chance, too!

❦

Does unceasing prayer and fellowship with the Father take priority in our everydays? Jesus gave prayer first place in His day, in His life, and Jesus is our example. While responsibilities to those we love must be met, our relationship to God, our responsibility to Him, must always come first. For with those we love we will walk but a mile. But with God, who is Love, we will walk an eternity.

Dwelling in the prayer-chapel of our hearts as we go about our day will develop within us a prayerful attitude. A prayerful attitude will prepare our hearts to hear God's call when He whispers to us. For the forever walk with God, the walk that lasts throughout eternity, begins the moment you and I decide to give Him our lives, all our earthly hours, and to wait at the mouth of the cave of our hearts to respond to His call that beckons us "come."

And when He calls, let us expect a surprise, for His soft voice will change our lives, no matter who we are, no matter where we are.

Do you remember Andrew and Simon, Zacchaeus and the nameless woman at the well? Christ's call changed their lives forever.

Christ looked for Andrew and Simon and found them fishing on the shores of a lake. "Come, Andrew. Come, Simon," Jesus called. And they followed Him and found a new vocation.

Christ looked for Zacchaeus and found him perched high in the limbs of a tree. "Come, Zacchaeus," Jesus called. And Zacchaeus climbed down and found a new heart.

Christ looked for a woman by a Samaritan well and found one shunned, without hope. "Come, dear one," Jesus called. And she drank from His cup of Living Water and found a new life.

Listen carefully, for in our noisiest hours, Christ may call to you, to me. He may call to us through the closeness of a grandmother's shoulder, the innocent face of an inner city child, a summer morning's gentle shower, fresh okra frying in a cast iron skillet, a hillside covered with tender young pines, a seashore alive with silver-winged seagulls, the miracle of a baby's birth, or a common spider that weaves her web outside our bedroom windows.

Listen, let us listen with the ears of our hearts, hearts prepared to hear God's voice. For it may come at unpredictable times, in unpredictable ways. Then let us follow . . . follow Him when He petitions us to come.

"The incredibly beautiful relationship between the Shepherd and His sheep can be and only is possible provided the sheep hear His voice, are known of Him in intimate oneness, and so follow Him in quiet, implicit confidence."[13]

❦

As we tarry in the chapel of our hearts, the relationship you and I now share with God will be enriched and strengthened with time . . . until that time, when we can step into the large old wardrobe . . . with its scent of cedar and its crunch of moth balls . . . where time no longer rules.

And when that time comes, let us enter Narnia with a smile on our lips and a twinkle in our eyes, for we can finally stay there, in that place that has no end, never again to leave.

QUESTIONS FOR GROUP STUDY

1. "Perhaps the visible world that seems so real, is not the real world at all, but simply a sort of "shadow-world," a shadow of the real world. Perhaps it is the world that is invisible, where we meet God in quiet privacy, where you

and I as believers in Christ will spend all eternity . . . perhaps this world, this world we cannot see, is truly the 'real world.'"

— Do you understand the full meaning of this statement? And, do you agree with it?

2. "It is the prepared heart that holds onto God's presence between the times of quiet solitude, between prayer-closet times."

— What is your opinion of that statement?

— List five ways we can prepare our hearts to "practice God's presence" between the times of the prayer-closet.

3. From within your own prayer-closet walls, what do you celebrate?

— List what you are most thankful for today.

— List what is most meaningful to you today.

— List those things you are most concerned about, those things that desperately need your prayers.

4. Do you agree with Henri Nouwen that "ceaseless interior prayer is a continual yearning of the human spirit towards God"?

— What does this statement mean to you?

— Has it tested true in your own life?

5. Do you believe that prayer is vital to our lives as Christian women today? Why? State several reasons.

6. Contemplate and discuss: "How can we spend a lifetime in prayer and fellowship with our Father when we have so much to do, so many places to go, so many needs to fulfill?"

– Name some ways not listed in the chapter, ways that you have found meaningful in your own life.

7. Is it realistic to believe that we, as busy Christian women, can learn to "pray without ceasing"? How?
– Share some meaningful and helpful ideas.

8. Reread Colossians 4:2. What does this verse say to us in regard to how and when we pray?

9. How can you and I follow Jesus' example and make prayer a priority in our lives?

10. Reread Mark 1:35, 6:46; Luke 5:16, 6:12, 9:28. What do these verses tell us about the practice of prayer in Jesus' life?

SUGGESTIONS FOR PERSONAL REFLECTION

Reread Psalm 66:18. Meditate upon the concept of forgiveness as described in this chapter by J. Oswald Sanders, in his book, *Spiritual Leadership*.
– Ask God to forgive your sins, the hidden ones as well as the visible ones.
– Pray that God will help you to forgive those who have mistreated or betrayed or abused you.
– Begin each prayer you pray asking God for His generous forgiveness.

8
...

The Servant's Heart

My friend, Scotti, only 33 years old, faints as she climbs stairs on a hot July day, and her nightmare begins.

A pastor's wife, Scotti has three children, a six-week-old baby, Jondelyn, a kindergartener, Scott, and an older daughter, Andrea. For no apparent reason, her blood pressure shoots up and her heart enlarges.

Final diagnosis: Primary Pulmonary Hypertension.

After several weeks of unsuccessful medical treatment, Scotti's doctor tells her he can do nothing more.

"How long will I live?" she asks.

He shakes his head. "Some people with PPH live six weeks; others can go on for several years. There's no way to know."

Scotti doesn't want to die. "I have so much left to do. I

117

want to see my children grow up. I love my husband Jon."

Jon takes the news hard. "Is there nothing, nothing at all we can do?" he asks the doctor.

The doctor gives him only one ray of hope. "There is the possibility that a heart and lung transplant can save her," he answers. "That is, if Scotti will agree to it and if we can find a donor."

Church members, family, and friends immediately encircle Scotti with prayer. Jon and Scotti fly to Pittsburgh, and put their name on the organ donor list there.

Eight months elapse.

No donor.

They drive to Birmingham and put their name on a second organ donor list. Then, with a multitude of those who love them, they pray, they wait, and they hope, as time ticks off like a broken clock.

A call comes from the hospital.

"Scotti, we have a heart/lung donor. Get everything ready to come today. Wait by the phone and I'll call you back."

Jon calls a deacon in their church, a former pilot, who has offered to arrange a private flight. With suitcase in hand, they wait and wait and wait. They wait all day by the phone. At 4:00 the call comes.

"I'm sorry, Scotti. The donor has an infection. We can't use his lungs."

Scotti's condition worsens as more time passes. Two years have passed since her doctor diagnosed PPH. No donor is in sight. But the prayers continue—urgent prayers—plead on behalf of Scotti.

On the morning of August 15, 1990, the Organ Transplant Coordinator from the University of Alabama Hospital calls again. "Scotti, we have a heart/lung donor. Get everything ready to come today."

Scotti places her hand over her failing heart. "Tonight,"

118

she says aloud, as if trying to make the almost unthinkable seem believable. "Tonight, I'll have a new heart and lungs."

Scotti barely has time to unpack her suitcase before the surgery begins. Lovingly, she takes out the photo of her family, the lace bookmark Scott made for her at Christmas, and the little wooden box Andrea gave her on her birthday, the birthday she thought might be her last.

The surgery goes well. But three weeks later, something happens. Scotti develops a viral infection, and her lungs fill with fluid.

The situation is serious. Her fluid-filled lungs can receive only 30 percent of the oxygen her body needs to sustain her life. Doctors can give her family no assurance that Scotti will live. The head resident comes into her room and prays with Scotti and Jon.

The church organizes a 24-hour-a-day prayer chain and prays ardently, unceasingly, for Scotti, as she lies in the hospital's Critical Intensive Care Unit.

They pray, they wait, they hope. And to the relief of all, a few days later Scotti's lungs begin to clear. Day after day, X-rays show a slight improvement, until sixty-six days after the surgery, Scotti is well enough to be released from the hospital. With a new heart and lungs, Scotti walks into the front door of her home on her thirty-sixth birthday, two weeks before Thanksgiving, eager to begin life anew.

"The experience has taught me to depend completely on God," Scotti recalls. "He showed His love through our church and family and friends who supported us continually with prayer. And God showed His love to us through an anonymous mother who, through the generous donation of her son's heart and lungs, turned his tragic death into the gift of new life, the gift that enabled this grateful mother to return home to her husband and children."

THE TRANSFORMED HEART

Scotti Doler was not the only one who received a new heart. Those faithful believers who prayed with her, for her, who so unselfishly held her for long months before the Father, also received new hearts, servants' hearts filled with love. Love unfathomable. The love, the heart, of Christ, Himself.

Prayers of intercession, prayed from the depths of our hearts, change our hearts. The natural heart, so preoccupied with self, transforms and becomes, instead, the heart engaged with others. The "self-oriented" heart matures into the "other-oriented" heart. The Shepherd's heart and our praying hearts become one, beating within our breasts on behalf of another who needs our prayers.

The self-giving servant cannot pray for another and, at the same time, maintain a selfish spirit. For the servant dies to self, the old self that lived only for self. She wants eagerly to give her new self to those whom Jesus loves, to those for whom Jesus has given Himself. When that happens, the natural heart, the selfish heart, is given the eyes of Christ, the gift of divine insight, and it can never again see the person in Earth's same dim light.

If the prayer of the struggling heart petitions God on behalf of the world's unknown others, the prayer of the servant's heart, the interceding heart, puts faces on those we hold in prayer. Intercessory prayer lifts to God, by name and need, those we envelop with prayer.

THE GIFT OF INTERCESSORY PRAYER

Not long ago, I heard a speaker deliver a moving speech urging the audience to join her crusade, a life-saving movement I whole-heartedly endorse.

But her final request disturbed me. She told us: "If you

cannot volunteer your time and energy to this great cause—
if you can't do anything else, then pray for us."

I have heard those same words spoken before by well-meaning believers. "If you can't do anything else . . . then pray."

Work, energy, time, money, blood, sweat, tears—nothing, *nothing* we can give another person can, in any way, equal the gift of service we give to them by praying for them. Intercessory prayer is the gift we give that remains unequaled in offering, in value.

When we pray for others, we show our love for our Savior, and we show our love for His sheep. No sweeter words can be said than those spoken to the Father on behalf of His child.

Whenever I close my eyes, I can see the slender form of my white-haired grandfather kneeling in prayer beside the plaid, family-room chair. It is one of my earliest and sweetest memories.

So regularly did he pray for others, the chair's cloth arm was worn bare in the spot where he placed his steadying hand.

My grandparents spent most of their prayer time praying for others. As a skinny, pig-tailed girl, I remember my grandfather telling me that they called my name "everyday in prayer."

As I grew up, married, had children, and dealt with a legion of decisions and pressures, I was always aware of, and comforted by, their loving petitions for me.

I now look back and realize that those were the dearest, most caring words Papa could ever say. Until his death in my thirty-sixth year, I always knew that no matter where in the world I was, no matter what situation I faced, no matter how I hurt or grieved, somewhere on a little farm in Rossville, Georgia, my grandparents were praying for me.

121

It brought me a comfort and strength that nothing else could.

Jesus said: "Love the Lord your God with all your heart and with all your soul and with all your mind and with all your strength. . . . [And] love your neighbor as yourself. There is no commandment greater than these." [1]

Intercessory prayer is the very heart of prayer, the prayer that not only blesses the one prayed for, but blesses the one who prays as well.

"We are never more like Christ than in prayers of intercession." [2]

Does Jesus, Himself, not call our hearts to become servants' hearts, hearts that kneel before God on behalf of others? The God of Creation humbled Himself to become one of us, to serve us, and He calls us to follow His self-giving example.

"The greatest among you should be like the youngest, and the one who rules like the one who serves. . . . I am among you as one who serves." [3]

How difficult is this servanthood concept for twentieth-century hearts! Our society instructs us to do the opposite: "Blessed is she," it teaches, "who is influential and strong, powerful and ambitious, commanding and controlling, assertive and self-assured."

"Dress for success!" it screams.

"Be Number One!" it advises.

"Climb your way to the top," it encourages, "no matter who you step on along the way!"

Yet, Jesus issues an even stronger command to you and me, one much more difficult to do:

"Serve," He says.

When Peter wanted to convey his love for Christ, he

stated boldly: "Lord, I am ready to go with You to prison and to death."[4]

But Jesus gave Peter a harder task to prove his love.

"Peter," Jesus said, "take care of My sheep; feed My lambs."[5]

What better way to take care of, to minister to, and to nourish, support, and sustain those whom Jesus loves, than to intercede for them in prayer?

"The effective, fervent prayer of a righteous man avails much," wrote the author of James.[6]

An effective prayer is a functional, practical prayer—a specific need requested of the Father.

A fervent prayer is an impassioned prayer—an intense, zealous, eager prayer. We cannot enter the prayer-closet to pray for another with our hearts unconcerned, indifferent, or listless. In the Garden of Gethsemane before Jesus faced the cross, so fervent was His prayer for you and me, that Luke, the physician, notes: "His sweat was like drops of blood falling to the ground."[7]

THE POEM OF PRAYER

Each night before I sleep, I lie in bed and study my "prayer wall" of photos. Some are new; some are old; some are faded with age. But each person is precious to me, and each receives a special prayer before I close my eyes.

I love the people who look to me from my bedside wall. I pray for them with thoughts of love; I pray for them by need and name. But, a lifetime of friendship and love, itself, cannot disclose the deepest needs of their hearts and souls. I can but know a few. The rest I must accept are known by God alone.

> For all those needs unknown to me,
> I ask that God will touch and tend,

God's Gentle Whisper

My silent prayers to Him I lift,
The One Who is all-knowing.[8]

You see, a person's life is like a poem. A living, breathing poem.

What is a poem? It is a collection of simple everyday words—carefully chosen words—a word here, a word there, each painting a portrait, each denoting a thought, each conveying a concept. In poetry, a word is worth a thousand pictures.

A poem is like a small town's junkyard that whispers its unwritten history by the bits and pieces it leaves behind. Bits and pieces as of a puzzle, a puzzle that speaks unspoken volumes to those who will listen, to those who will look.

We listen and we see . . .

A rusted tricycle and the life of a man who, as a toddler, once rode upon it . . .

A pair of worn crutches and a tired old veteran with a wealth of war tales, remembered and shared . . .

A dog-eared cookbook and a mother's devotion as day after day she loves and feeds those who gather at her table.

Such is a person like a poem. When we walk through a person's life, carefully and slowly, we see the puzzle of bits and pieces—bits of love and joy, pieces of hurt and sorrow. By listening, by looking, we can read volumes unspoken.

We listen and we see . . .

The rusted tricycle of the child she never had . . .

The worn crutches of a dream she had to forfeit . . .

The dog-eared cookbook of a love she found and lost.

For each person's life is lived full and empty. And we are given but a stanza, never the full verse of her life.

But God knows her heart, in and out and throughout the sonnet of her soul. He knows every thought, every fear, every desire. He knows her gain and loss, her hope and dream, her secret love. He knows the ballad of her heart as He knows His own heart, without secret, without pretense, without the masquerade of a self-concealing mask.

Thus, we hold the face of the one we love before us, within our secret chambers. With words unspoken, but with words impassioned, we place this living, breathing poem of life at the faithful Father's feet.

Surely, "the real business of [our] life as a saved soul is intercessory prayer," the "ministry of the interior."[9]

❦

"If your heart is as My heart, then give Me your hand."[10] Let us, together, hear anew Christ's words to me, to you.

"Take care of My sheep."

"Feed My lambs."

And when we care for, and when we feed those he entrusts, through prayer, to us . . . we will be given new hearts, servants' hearts filled with love. Love unfathomable. The love, the heart, of Christ, Himself.

QUESTIONS FOR GROUP STUDY

1. Ponder this statement about intercessory prayer: "Prayers of intercession, prayed from the depths of our hearts, change our hearts. The natural heart, so preoccupied with self, transforms and becomes, instead, the heart engaged with others."

   – Have you found this statement to be true?

2. Consider the word *transformation*. What does it mean to you?

– Have you experienced a transforming time in your own life that you can share with a friend or group?

3. Describe the difference between these two prayers: The prayer of the struggling heart and the prayer of the servant's heart.

4. "Work, energy, time, money, blood, sweat, tears— nothing, nothing we can give another person can, in any way, equal the gift of service we give to them by praying for them. Intercessory prayer is the gift we give that remains unequaled in offering, in value."
– Do you regard the worth of intercessory prayer to be this vital to the Christian life? Why or why not?

5. "We are never more like Christ than in prayers of intercession."
– How do our prayers, by need and name, for others help us to become more like Christ? Discuss.

6. Can you describe in as few words as possible the meaning of *the servant's heart.*

7. Read John 21:15-17. What do these verses mean to you?

8. This chapter compares a person's life to a poem. Can you think of other ways to describe a person's life as it relates to intercessory prayer?

9. Do you agree with this statement by Oswald Chambers concerning intercessory prayer: "The real business of [our] life as a saved soul is intercessory prayer"?

SUGGESTIONS FOR PERSONAL REFLECTION

In your quiet time, reread John 14:13-14 and meditate upon its meaning and its promise.

Contemplate deeply Mark 11:24. Then pray for those you know and love, by name and need, with the promise of God in your heart that He will hear and answer your prayers prayed on behalf of others.

Set aside a certain time each day to pray specifically for the needs of others. To pray the prayer without words, here are some suggestions:

– Write down your prayer request on a slip of paper. Then place it, along with others, in a small box. Daily, in your quiet time, reread the prayer requests you've written. After a certain amount of time has passed, go through the box and note the answered prayers.

– Keep a photo of those you pray for daily. Look at the photo as you think about and pray for that particular person. Ask God to lead you to pray for that person according to his or her present need.

– When an intercessory prayer need is urgent, write the need on a card and attach to your cabinet or refrigerator or desk or dashboard. During the day, use the card as a constant reminder to pray frequently for this person and her particular need.

– After you pray a prayer of intercession, consider writing a note to the person you have prayed for. Let her know of your prayers and love for her.

– As you pray for another, envision in your mind that the person for whom you are praying is kneeling and joining you in prayer.

9
...

The Shepherd's Heart

John Griffin adores his eight-year-old son, Greg. Father and son, they look alike, they walk alike, and they talk alike—of ships and seas and exotic places they will one day sail together. John's wife smiles as she listens to them dream aloud, long into the night, of faraway fantastic places.

On this warm spring day in 1937, John, the operator of one of the major railway drawbridges that crosses the Mississippi River, brings Greg to work with him. For the very first time, Greg watches with excitement as his father pulls a lever and raises the giant bridge to let a ship pass through. Then, with equal enthusiasm, Greg watches his father pull the lever that lowers the bridge to let a train pass over.

God's Gentle Whisper

At noon, John raises the bridge and lets a ship pass through. Then he pats his son on the back. "There won't be a train for a while," he tells Greg. "Want to see the deck?"

Greg shouts a hearty "yes," and father and son walk a few hundred feet down the catwalk and eat sack lunches on the bridge observation deck.

A golden sun warms the air and a gentle wind breezes along the river as John and Greg look out upon the water and talk of the magical places the ships might sail. Time stands still as father and son enjoy each other's company.

Suddenly, a sharp distant whistle startles their thoughts. John jumps to his feet and looks at his watch. The Memphis Express, the train that passes each day at 1:07, is speeding down the railway track . . . and the bridge is raised!

"Stay here, Greg!" John shouts and races down the catwalk, climbs the ladder, and rushes into the control booth.

"Four hundred passengers are on that train," he mutters to himself as he quickly places his hand on the lever to lower the mighty bridge. But just as he begins to pull the lever, he sees a horrible sight.

"Greg!" he screams. But Greg can't move. The young boy has tried to follow his dad. But he has slipped and fallen. Greg's left leg is firmly lodged in the gigantic gear box that operates the drawbridge.

John freezes. He knows that if he pulls the lever to lower the bridge, tons of grinding steel will slowly chew and crush Greg's small body. But he also knows that if he doesn't pull the lever, 400 passengers abroad the Memphis Express will be hurled to their deaths in the river below.

John sees a rope hanging in the corner of the control booth. "Will it work?" he asks himself.

Gripped by panic, John plans his son's rescue. If only he can reach his son in time, he can use the rope to lower himself into the gears, free his son, climb back up the rope, race back to the control booth, and pull the lever.

John grabs the rope and scurries down the first few steps of the ladder toward his son. Then John hears the high-pitched train whistle again, shrieking much louder than before, now much closer than he had thought.

Too close to rescue his son.

His heart stabs with pain, his eyes fill with tears. Oh, how he loves his boy, his only son, caught beneath him in the drawbridge gears. But he knows only one thing to do. Four hundred passengers will be speeding across the track any second, and they are depending on John to have the drawbridge safely lowered, to deliver them from instant destruction.

John buries his face into his arm and pulls the lever. As the great drawbridge lowers slowly into place, John hears the agonizing cries of his son as the monstrous gear box grinds Greg to death.

Painfully, John lifts his face and looks at the passengers aboard the train that his precious son has given his life to save. Some read the daily newspaper, completely unaware of John. Others chat and drink coffee in the dining car, oblivious even to the crossing of the bridge. Some children laugh and play happily with trinkets and toys. Only a few passengers look John's way, extend their hand, and smile a heartfelt smile that says, "thank you."

No one sees the tears on John's face. No one notices the small crushed body in the gear box below. And no one guesses the price just paid so that they might cross the river safely.

To most of the passengers aboard the Memphis Express, it's just another day, just another crossing.[1]

131

THE COST TO GOD

When I first heard this true story of John Griffin and his son Greg, I felt like a nine-year-old girl again, sitting at my grandfather's feet, listening to him read from the big black Bible he held on his lap.

"For God so loved the world that He gave His only begotten Son. . . ."

"God loved *you* so much, 'Nisey. . . ." Papa stopped reading to tell me, "That He gave His only Son, Jesus . . .

"That whoever believes in Him should not perish but have everlasting life."[2] He finished reading and then focused his clear sky-blue eyes on mine.

And that hot afternoon in August, the verse he read to me changed my life. Forever.

Truly, the privilege of prayer comes not without a great cost to the Father, a great cost to His Son.

For God, the Father, looked down on that warm spring day, 2000 years ago, and His heart stabbed with pain, His eyes filled with tears.

Oh, how He loved His boy, His only Son, arrested by soldiers, spit upon, and mocked. But there was only one thing to do. For a world of people were speeding through time and space, passing through the centuries, and they were depending on him to save them from eternal destruction.

So the Father buried His face in His arm and allowed the executioner to hammer the nails into His Son's frail body. As the cross was lifted and lodged into the ground, God heard the agonizing cries of His Son, as Jesus hung by nailed hands and feet and died a slow death.

And the passengers aboard Planet Earth? Some read the daily newspaper . . . others chatted and drank coffee in the dining car . . . some children laughed and played happily with trinkets and toys. Only a few looked God's way, extended their hand, and smiled a heartfelt smile that said, "Thank you."

No one saw the tears on God's face. Few noticed or remembered the crushed bruised body upon that wooden cross. And no one guessed the price just paid so that they might cross the River safely.

To most of the passengers aboard Planet Earth, it was just another day, just another crossing.

❦

The privilege to pray came at great cost. Oh, that you and I will never allow this phenomenon of prayer to become a route to ritual, a lukewarm litany, or a half-hearted behest made as by a customer to an ecclesiastical bellhop! Prayer is too priceless, too precious, to be put off, to be unappreciated. For the believer in Christ, prayer is the very beat of her heart, the next breath of air she will breathe, the center of her thoughts, desires, and deep affections. Prayer is the gift of Christ, Himself, a gift He willingly gives, a prize to cherish, an opportunity to extend our hands to Him. Slip out of Shadow-World and step into the presence of God Almighty—the One who loves us, the One who gave Himself for us, the One who, even now, prays for us.

THE HOLY SPIRIT—OUR TEACHER

"The One who, even now, prays for us. . . ."

Insight visited me one early quiet morning as I sat in my secret place and waited in prayer. This never-before dawned insight has since given me new understanding in my prayer life. So simple yet so profound, so apparent yet so imperceptible, the insight is this:

I do not know how to pray.

The acknowledgment of such inability frightens me and

133

terribly humbles me. For I am like a little child who stands before my heavenly parent with selfish babblings and immature wants. I am a limited human being, a woman who truly loves the Lord and has given herself to Him, yet prayer lies so beyond my human capacity to understand, to faithfully and properly practice without help.

I am reminded of the difficult delivery of my first child, my only son, Christian. Two weeks overdue—hot August weeks—weeks that gave new meaning to the word "waiting"—Christian was an impatient package of eager new life, yet unable to be born without help. So, to aid me with the birth, a skilled surgeon sliced open with ease my protruding abdomen, lifting from me that which I could not deliver alone. In doing so, the gifted helper gave my son "wings"—the ability to breathe with his own lungs, the power to take on life that lived beyond me.

The analogy is a rather crude one, but prayer is somewhat like that C-Section I underwent over a decade ago. The prayers that live within my heart are like impatient packages of new life, eager to make themselves known to the Father. Yet, I need One greater than I, the gifted Helper, to deliver to God that which I cannot alone deliver. I need assistance to lift from me my heart's petitions and make them acceptable to approach the Almighty's ears.

Therefore . . .

God provides One greater than I to teach me how to pray. God fills my whole being with Himself, the Holy Spirit, my Teacher, my Helper, my lifelong Guide. And I no longer pray with selfish babblings and immature wants. I pray a prayer with beauty and grace, a prayer uttered for me by the One who knows the heart of God, by the one who knows how to pray, by the One who gives my prayers "wings" so that they might live apart from me and so fill the Father's heart.

THE MYSTERY OF THE TRINITY

And when my prayers reach God's ears, He reaches out and wraps His gentle arms around me. For I am His, the one He loves, the child who takes her first awkward steps in pursuit of walking a lifetime in prayerful communion with Him.

Can you and I ever understand the mystery of the Trinity that enables us to pray?

Of God the Father, Who hears our prayers and Who responds to our petitions,

Of God the Son, Who willingly gave His life to reconcile us to the Father, and to grant us the privilege of prayer,

And of God the Holy Spirit, Who helps us pray those prayers we cannot plead alone?

Such is the power of God the Father in our lives, redeeming us through God the Son, reforming us through God the Holy Spirit. *God* the Holy Spirit prays on our behalf to *God* the Father in the name of the One who made prayer possible, *God* the Son.

Deep calls unto deep, and I confess to you, the mystery of prayer is beyond my comprehension. I do not know how to pray. I will forever need the Helper to free within me those prayers that struggle to be born.

Perhaps the only prayer I can truly pray is the prayer of the publican in Luke 18:13. Like he, with bowed head and bowed heart, I beg: "God, have mercy on me, a sinner."

It's humbling, to be sure, but I believe this is the way to approach the Father, for this prayer is prayed without fear of an intruding arrogance or pride or self-righteouness. It is a prayer that can only be prayed with an appreciative heart, a grateful heart, a humble heart, for I owe God a debt that I can never repay.

I agree with D. T. Niles when he said we are all just

beggars telling one another where to find bread.

How beautiful is the love of God that He so heartily embraces us beggars and envelops us with a love beyond the grasp of words to describe.

PRICELESS, PRECIOUS PRAYER

So it is with first-step clumsiness, a mere toddler's try at walking, that I lift my heart and open it wide, giving God my love, receiving His love, and, with the Holy Spirit's help, approach my Father in prayer.

And I discover anew . . .

The prayer of the waiting heart, the prayer that cannot be rushed, the prayer that needs time to think, to ponder, to brood, to watch, to listen. The prayer that "stands under, in active strength, enduring till the answer comes."

The prayer of the struggling heart, the prayer that falls on bended knee to the Creator of all humankind, beseeching, pleading, begging on behalf of the world's unknown others who hurt and hunger and sorrow and grieve, the world's little lambs who have yet to respond to the loving Shepherd's heart.

The prayer of the expectant heart, the prayer that waits on tiptoe, wide-eyed and curious, expecting a surprise from the One Who whispers when we expect Him to shout, from the One Who shouts when we expect Him to whisper.

The prayer of the prepared heart, the prayer that keeps praying while riding 'round and 'round the merry-go-round of life. The prayer that listens always for the Father's voice amidst the chaos and noise and confusion of Shadow-World society.

The prayer of the servant's heart, the prayer that prays by name and need, the prayer that intercedes for those whose faces grace the bedside wall.

The prayer of the Shepherd's heart, the prayer Christ

prays on our behalf, the gift of prayer that Christ purchased for you, for me, on a warm spring day on a wooden cross.

Priceless, precious prayer is a secret, yours and mine, to be enjoyed, to be planned, to be anticipated, throughout our days, throughout our lives. For our hours of solitude, our still hours, are sacred hours, not to be spent carelessly, but to be used carefully, to be cherished, sought, savored, shared.

How ironic that you and I, as believers in Christ, seek the solitude that society shuns, pursue the silence from which humankind runs to escape, embrace the aloneness from which the world swiftly flees and outright labels loneliness.

Share the secret.

Solitude, silence, aloneness—so vital to, so treasured by, the one who prays; so strange, so frightening to the one who doesn't, to the one who strays.

❦

There are so many ways to pray. So many ways to fellowship with our Father. The ways to pray are as distinctive as you and I, a world of Christ-devoted women with personalities and talents so beautifully varied. Yet, we each hold dear the secret that makes us sisters—our "yes" to the Shepherd's love, our response to the Shepherd's sacrifice, our closeness to the Shepherd's heart.

Prayer—wonderful, beautiful prayer . . . what a gift, what a privilege!

Sometimes I need to sing and dance and clap my hands as David did when he offered his prayers of thanksgiving to God before the Ark of the Lord.[3] How often can my body speak the language of joy unknown to rigid words.

Sometimes I need to feel the hurt that cuts my heart in

two, to cry the tears God saves of mine, to let my prayer be one of pain, a pain too deep for words.

Sometimes I need to walk again the road that leads to Calvary, to pray my words of gratitude. Yet I need words so lovely to the ear, so rich to the heart, that language, itself, does not contain them. So my heart must speak within itself those words not yet discovered.

Surely, my heart yearns for that which I cannot put into words, that which my limited language cannot express. Otherwise, how shallow my prayers would be if they were restricted to the concrete walls of my imprisoned vocabulary. The prayer from the very depths of my heart is a prayer unspeakable, a prayer full of thanks and joy, dance and tears, song and sorrow.

Surely, the gift of prayer is so full of potential and promise, so blessed by a woman's unique individual expression, the Holy Spirit will never allow it to settle into predictable patterns.

Our prayers must take on the newness that each morning brings to our Christ-devoted hearts. For each day is presented to us pregnant with surprise, expectation, and discovery. Just as the old Indian once placed his foot in a river's stream, he could not place it there again within the stream's same spot.

So . . . today in prayer we dance and sing, tomorrow we sigh and cry. Each day blesses us singularly, for the river never ceases to flow and time leaves us standing each day within a different stream.

"But thou, when thou prayest, enter into thy closet, and when thou hast shut thy door, pray to thy Father which is in secret."[4]

When I hear that verse, I remember Mama, my beloved grandmother, for Mama spent much time in her closet secreted with the Father. In fact, her entire life was a prayer.

Surely, every heart must have its hush, to wait and listen in sacred solitude, to go out and stand on the mountaintop, to "be still and know that I am God."

More than anyone else, Mama taught me the value and beauty of a secret place and a prayer of waiting and listening to the still, small voice that whispers within the prayer-closet walls.

Oh, that I could know God like Elijah and Mama knew him!

JESUS, ELIJAH AND MOSES

We meet Elijah one more time before the scriptures close. He stands again on a mountaintop, this time with Jesus and Moses. The mountains are not unknown by these three men, for they have spent much time upon the hills in prayer.

Three disciples, Peter, James, and John, watch, and rub their eyes in disbelief when Jesus' robes become white with blinding light, and there appears with him two prophets from the past. "Please stay," they urge, and offer to build houses where they might dwell.

But, years ago, Moses had to leave the mountaintop to deliver tablets of stone.

Years ago, Elijah, too, had to climb down and stand at the mouth of the cave, awaiting instructions from God for the work he was to do.

For their waiting, listening hearts had heard the Whisper, and their hearts were changed and opened and eager to obey.

And, now, Peter, James, and John. Jesus cannot stay upon the mountaintop either, for the world's stray lambs are lost in a thicket dense, and the Shepherd must go to rescue His flock and save them from the dark night's wolves.

For once we hear God's gentle whisper, we can no longer remain on the mountaintop; we must come down, and we must obey.

QUESTIONS FOR GROUP STUDY

1. What verse of Scripture is most meaningful to you?
   – Has a single verse of scripture made such an impact on your life that it changed your life? Share the scripture with a friend, or with a group.

2. "Truly, the privilege of prayer comes not without a great cost to the Father, a great cost to His Son."
   – Silently ponder the great price paid by the Father and the Son for our salvation.
   – Offer God a heartfelt prayer of gratitude as you reflect on His love and His sacrifice for you.

3. Do you agree with the following statement: "I do not know how to pray"?
   – What is meant by this statement?
   – Do you find it to be true in your own life? Why?

4. Reread this statement and respond as a group to its meaning: "*God* the Holy Spirit prays on our behalf to *God* the Father in the name of the One who made prayer possible, *God* the Son."

5. Meditate on the words of D. T. Niles: "We are all just beggars telling one another where to find bread."
   – What does this image say to you?
   – Do you agree or disagree?

140

6. One by one, examine the following types of prayers:
  – The prayer of the waiting heart
  – The prayer of the struggling heart
  – The prayer of the expectant heart
  – The praycr of the prepared heart
  – The prayer of the servant's heart
  – The prayer of the Shepherd's heart
  – What do they mean to you?
  – What do they mean to your own personal prayer life?

7. What are some of the ways you find most meaningful to pray? List them and discuss them as a group.

8. Reread Romans 8:26-27. What is the work of the Holy Spirit in our prayers, in our lives? Discuss.

SUGGESTIONS FOR PERSONAL REFLECTION

Reread I Corinthians 4:7 and James 1:17. Contemplate their meanings. Why is it essential that we pray special prayers of thanksgiving to God for the gifts He has given us? Why should we
– Thank Him for those gifts for which we are most grateful?
– Distinguish within ourselves those gifts that are temporary and those gifts that are eternal?
– Pray that we can receive, use, and give to others those gifts He gives to us?

Read John 14:26, 16:8 and Romans 8:9. Ask God to grant you keener understanding of His Holy Spirit as He works in your life. Plan a special time of devotions and reflect on your personal experience with Jesus Christ. Ask yourself these questions:

– Have I become a new creature since I gave my life to the Lord? In what ways have I changed? In what ways do I need to change?

– How can regular and frequent prayer transform me to the image of Christ? How can I better follow the example of prayer Jesus taught in Scripture?

– How can frequent prayer protect me from the Evil One? How can I become less vulnerable to Satan and to temptation by staying close to God in prayer? (Reread Proverbs 4:14-15, Matthew 26:41, I Corinthians 10:13, Hebrews 12:1, James 1:12-15, and I John 5:18-19.)

Reread and ponder the words of praise offered by David in I Chronicles 29:10-13. How does David's act of praise speak to you in regard to personal worship?

Reread Revelation 5:13, 11:15. Contemplate the eternal kingdom, power, and glory of the Lord as you reflect upon these verses.

Please use the following Scripture references, questions, comments, and suggestions for a more intensive, probing group study, and/or for deeper personal contemplation.

1. For scriptures regarding the Trinity, reread Genesis 1:2; Deuteronomy 6:4; Psalm 33:6, 9, 104:30, 107:20; Proverbs 3:19, 8:1-36; John 1:1-4; and Zechariah 4:6.

– Also read Matthew 3:3-17, 28:19; Mark 1:9-11; Luke 3:21-22; John 14:16, 15:26, 16:13-15; I Corinthians 12:3-6; II Corinthians 13:14; Galatians 4:4-6; Ephesians 4:4-6; I Peter 1:2; and Revelation 1:4.

– Then, using the Scripture references above, respond to the following four statements:

– God is One.

– God has three distinct ways of being in the redemptive event, however He remains an undivided unity.

– We can grasp the concept of the Trinity through the threefold participation in salvation.

– The Trinity is a mystery we cannot adequately explain or, with human mind, fully understand.

– Discuss the role that the Trinity plays in our prayers today.

2. Who is Jesus Christ, and what is the significance of
   – His preexistence: (See John 1:1)?

– His conception and birth: (See the beginning chapters of Matthew and Luke)?

– His crucifixion, death, and burial: (See Luke 23:50-56, John 19:38-42, Acts 1-12, and Galatians 3)?

– His resurrection: (See Matthew 27:56, 61, 28:1-2, 16-20; Mark 16; Luke 24:13-32, 34, 36-43; John 20:11-18, 24-29; Acts 9:1-9; and I Corinthians 15:3-8.)

– Where is Jesus Christ now, and what is His work in regards to our lives, to our prayer lives? (See Matthew 26:64, Mark 14:62, and Luke 22:69.)

3. Reread II Timothy 3:16 and describe the work of the Holy Spirit in the Bible, God's Word.

– What role does the Holy Spirit take as far as helping us to understand the Scriptures and their deeper meaning and implications?

– Regarding the Bible today, do you agree with this statement: "The Bible has no rival in its pervasive influence upon Western culture, and increasingly over world culture?"

– What do you see as the role and the importance of the Bible in today's society/world?

143

4. Using only the parables of Jesus, describe the conversion experience that redeems us and guarantees us life everlasting:

– Sin: (See Matthew 22:2-9 and Luke 14:16-23, "The Marriage Supper.")

– Jesus Christ: (See John 10:1-16, "The Good Samaritan.")

– Conviction: (See Luke 7:41, "The Prayer of the Convicted.")

– Repentance: (See Matthew 7:14 and Luke 13:24, "The Narrow Gate.")

– God's forgiveness: (See Matthew 18:23-35, "Two Debtors.")

– God's acceptance: (See Luke 10:30-37, "The Good Samaritan.")

– Perseverance in prayer: (See Luke 18:2-5, "The Widow.")

– Humility in prayer: (See Luke 18:10-14, "The Pharisee and Tax-gatherer.")

5. Reread and discuss the following scriptures regarding the gifts of the Holy Spirit: Exodus 31:2-3; Judges 3:9-10, 6:34, 14:6,19; I Samuel 10:6; Micah 3:8; Mark 1:10, 13:11; Luke 4:14-18, 11:13; Acts 2:1-47, 2:3-4, 17-18, 38; Romans 8:9; I Corinthians 12:4-7, 31–13:1; and I Peter 4:10.

6. Ponder Christ's redemptive work as it regards healing of spirit, soul, and body. How does knowledge of His redemptive work affect and change our prayers?

7. Reread Matthew 28:19-20.

– What does evangelism and sharing the gospel of Christ mean to you?

– How can you personally, and through a larger group, tell a hurting, lost world about the redemptive work of Jesus Christ?

– How does prayer aid our evangelistic efforts?

8. Ponder the following Scripture references: Matthew 16:18, 18:17; Acts 2:47, 14:23; I Corinthians 11:22, 15:9; Ephesians 1:22, 3:10, 5:25, 27, 29; Philippians 4:15; Colossians 1:24; I Timothy 3:15, 5:16; Hebrews 12:23, and Revelation 2:1.

– What do these verses tell you about the Church?

– What is our responsibility to the Body of Christ, the Church?

– How does our personal prayer life influence our fellowship and worship with other believers?

– Why is worship, both personal and corporate, important?

– What place does prayer hold in corporate worship services?

9. Reread Matthew 24-25, Mark 13, John 14:3, Acts 1:11, and Titus 2:13.

– What do these verses of scripture say to you about the personal return of Jesus Christ?

– In what ways can we prepare our hearts for His coming?

– What role does personal prayer play in regard to the biblical teaching on the return of Jesus to earth at the end of earthly history?

– How can we be watchful and alert (Matthew 24:42, 25:1-13; and II Peter 3:3-4)?

– How can we best use our time before His coming (Colossians 3:1-17; I Thessalonians 3:13; and I John 2:28, 3:3)?

Source Notes

CHAPTER ONE

1. Matthew 6:6.

2. C. S. Lewis, *The Problem with Pain* (London, England: Fontana, 1940), p. 93.

3. Oswald Chambers, *If You Will Ask* (Grand Rapids, MI: Discovery House Publishers, 1958), p. 36.

4. Hebrews 1:1-2.

5. Hebrews 11:6.

6. J. I. Packer, *Knowing God* (Downers Grover, IL: InterVarsity Press, 1973), pp. 14-15.

7. Psalm 46:10.

8. Matthew 6:6 (KJV)

CHAPTER TWO

1. Psalm 42:1-2 RSV.
2. St. Augustine, *Confessions* (Middlesex, England: Penguin, 1961), p. 21.
3. Matthew 7:7-8.
4. Mark 6:53-55.
5. Matthew 18:12 NCV.
6. Mark 4:3-5.
7. Matthew 6:28-29 NCV.
8. Max Lucado, *The Applause of Heaven* (Dallas, TX: Word Publishing, 1990), pp. 22-23.

CHAPTER THREE

1. Genesis 3:15 NKJV.
2. See Galatians 4:4.
3. John Bunyan, *The Pilgrim's Progress* (Old Tappan, NJ: Fleming H. Revell Co., 1974 [originally published 1688]), p. 35.
4. Verna Birkey, *If God Is In Control, Why Is My World Falling Apart?* (Portland, OR: Multnomah, 1990), p. 93.
5. Job 23:3, 8, 9 NKJV.
6. Psalm 28:1, 2.
7. Lamentations 3:7, 8.
8. Lamentations 5:20.
9. I Kings 19:4.
10. Matthew 27:46.
11. Max Lucado, *Six Hours One Friday* (Portland, OR: Multnomah Press, 1989), p. 23.
12. Oswald Chambers, *My Utmost for His Highest* (New York: Dodd, Mead, and Company, 1935), p. 7.
13. Psalm 40:1-3.

14. Lamentations 3:25-26, my emphasis.

15. Jeremiah 29:12-13.

16. Chambers, *My Utmost for His Highest*, p. 285.

17. Birkey, *If God Is In Control, Why Is My World Falling Apart?*, p. 93.

18. Chambers, *My Utmost for His Highest*, p. 285.

19. Psalm 37:7.

20. Lucado, *Six Hours One Friday*, p. 161.

CHAPTER FOUR

1. Mark 1:35 NCV.

2. Catherine Marshall, *Light in My Darkest Night* (Old Tappan, NJ: Chosen Books, 1989), p. 211.

3. Ibid., p. 231.

4. Warren W. Wiersbe, *Five Secrets of Living* (Wheaton, IL: Living Books, 1977), p. 83.

5. Phillip Keller, *A Shepherd Looks at The Good Shepherd and His Sheep* (Grand Rapids, MI: Zondervan Publishing House, 1978), p. 108.

6. Ray Burwick, *Self-Esteem: You're Better Than You Think* (Wheaton, IL: Tyndale House Publishers, Inc., 1983), p. 79.

7. Wiersbe, p. 42.

8. Ibid., p. 42.

9. Ecclesiastes 1:1-4, 8, 9 NCV.

10. Warren W. Wiersbe, *Be Satisfied* (Wheaton, IL: Victor Books, 1990), p. 21. (Paraphrased)

11. I John 2:15-17 NCV.

12. Wiersbe, *Be Satisfied*, Foreword.

13. John 10:10 NCV.

14. Elisabeth Elliot, *Trusting God in a Twisted World* (Old Tappan, NJ: Fleming H. Revell Co., 1989), p. 127.

15. Warren W. Wiersbe, *In Praise of Plodders!* (Grand

Rapids, MI: Kregel Publications. 1991), p. 77.

16. Ferdinand W. Blanchard, "Word of God, Across the Ages," *The Baptist Hymnal* (Nashville, TN: Convention Press, 1975 edition), p. 148.

17. Chambers, *If You Will Ask*, p. 39.

CHAPTER FIVE

1. W. Phillip Keller, *Sea Edge* (Waco, TX: Word Publishing, 1985), p. 99.

2. Henri J. M. Nouwen, *The Way of the Heart* (New York: Ballantine Books, 1981), p. 24.

3. I Kings 18:41-46.

4. Genesis 18:23-33.

5. Luke 11:9.

6. Nouwen, p. 22.

7. Attributed to Oscar Wilde.

8. See I Kings 18:20-40.

CHAPTER SIX

1. Max Lucado, *The Applause of Heaven* (Dallas, TX: Word Publishing, 1990), p. 190.

2. Luke 23.34.

3. John 19:30.

CHAPTER SEVEN

1. C. S. Lewis, *The Chronicles of Narnia: The Lion, the Witch and the Wardrobe* (New York: Collier Books, 1950).

2. Brother Lawrence, *The Practice of the Presence of God* (Springdale, PA: Whitaker House, 1982), p. 46.

3. Henri J. M. Nouwen, *The Way of the Heart* (New York: Ballantine Books, 1981), pp. 67, 68.

4. Martin Luther.

5. I Thessalonians 5:17.

6. Mark 6:31.

7. Matthew Henry, "A Method for Prayer" (Chester, MA:[copy of original pamphlet dated March 25, 1710]).

8. J. Oswald Sanders, *Spiritual Leadership* (Chicago, IL: Moody Press, 1967/1980), p. 106.

9. Lucado, *The Applause of Heaven*, p. 23.

10. Keller, *A Shepherd Looks at The Good Shepherd and His Sheep*, p. 171.

11. Philippians 4:8 NKJV.

12. Sanders, p. 163.

13. Keller, *A Shepherd Looks at The Good Shepherd and His Sheep*, p. 165

CHAPTER EIGHT

1. Mark 12:30-31.

2. Austin Phelps, *The Still Hours* (Carlisle, PA: The Banner of Truth Trust, 1974 [first published in 1859]), p. 80.

3. Luke 22:26-27.

4. Luke 22:33.

5. Paraphrased: See John 21:15-17.

6. James 5:16 NKJV.

7. Luke 22:44 (See Luke 22:39-53).

8. Denise George.

9. Chambers, *If You Will Ask*, p. 172.

10. Phrase quoted by John Wesley.

CHAPTER NINE

1. I first heard this story told by Adolph Coors IV, Shades Mountain Baptist Church, 1991. (I have paraphrased it.)

2. John 3:16 NKJV.

3. II Samuel 6:14.

4. Matthew 6:6.

Support Groups– Places of Growth and Healing

Women are hungry for teaching and nurturing as they grapple with issues that touch them where they live—loss, self-worth, singleness, remarriage, and numerous other felt needs.

God's heart is to heal and restore his people. In fact, Jesus states this clearly in Luke 4:18, 19 when he announces that God has called him to minister to the oppressed, the hurting, and the brokenhearted. We read throughout the entire New Testament how he wants to equip the Body of Christ to join him in reaching out in love and support of the bruised and wounded. Support groups provide this special place where healing can happen—where women are given time and space to be open about themselves in the context of loving acceptance and honest caring.

WHAT IS A SUPPORT GROUP?

• A support group is a small-group setting which offers women a "safe place." The recommended size is from eight to ten people.

• It is a compassionate, nonthreatening, confidential place where women can be open about their struggles and receive caring and support in a biblically-based, Christ-centered atmosphere.

• It is an accepting place, where women are listened to and loved right where they are.

• It is a place where love and truth are shared and the Holy Spirit is present to bring God's healing.

• It is a place where women learn to take responsibility for making Christ-like choices in their own lives.

• A support group has designated leadership. Co-leaders are strongly recommended to share the role of facilitators.

• It is a cohesive and consistent group. This implies "closing" it to additional participants after the second or third meeting before beginning with a new topic.

WHAT SUPPORT GROUPS ARE NOT

• They are not counseling groups.

• They are not places to "fix" or change women.

• They are not Bible study or prayer groups as such, although Scripture and prayer are a natural framework for the meetings.

• They are not places where women concentrate on themselves and "stay there." Instead they provide opportunity to grow in self-responsibility and wholeness in Christ.

Small groups often rotate leadership among participants, but because support groups usually meet for a specific time period with a specific mutual issue, it works well for a team of co-leaders to be responsible for the meetings. As you can see, leadership is important! Let's take a look at it.

WHAT ARE THE PERSONAL LEADERSHIP QUALIFICATIONS OF A SUPPORT GROUP LEADER?

Courage (1 Cor. 16:13, 14)

A leader shows courage in the following ways in her willingness to:

• Be open to self-disclosure, admitting her own mistakes and taking the same risks she expects others to take.

• Lovingly explore areas of struggle with women, and look beyond their behavior to hear what's in their hearts.

• Be secure in her own beliefs, sensitive to the Holy Spirit's promptings, and willing to act upon them.

• Draw on her own experiences to help her identify with others in the group and be emotionally touched by them.

• Consistently examine her own life in the light of God's Word and the Holy Spirit's promptings.

• Be direct and honest with members, not use her role to protect herself from interaction with the group.

• Know that wholeness is the goal and that change is a process.

Willingness to Model (Ps. 139:23, 24)

• A group leader should have had moderate victory in her own struggles, with adequate healing having taken place. If she is not whole in the area she is leading, she should at least be fully aware of her unhealed areas and not be defensive of them. She should be open to those who can show her if she is misguiding others by ministering out of her own hurt.

155

• She understands that group leaders lead largely by example, by doing what she expects members to do.

• She is no longer "at war" with her past and can be compassionate to those who may have victimized her. Yet she is a "warrior woman," strong in her resistance of Satan with a desire to see other captives set free.

Presence (Gal. 6:2)

• A group leader needs to either have had personal experience with a support group or observed enough so she understands how they function.

• A group leader needs to be emotionally present with the group members, being touched by others' pain, struggles, and joys.

• She needs to be in touch with her own feelings so that she can have compassion for and empathy with the other women.

• She must understand that her role is as a facilitator. She is not to be the answer person nor is she responsible for change in others. Yet she must be able to evidence leadership qualities that enable her to gather a group around her.

Goodwill and Caring (Matt. 22:27, 28)

• A group leader needs to express genuine caring, even for those who are not easy to care for. That takes a commitment to love and a sensitivity to the Holy Spirit.

• She should be able to express caring by (1) inviting women to participate but allowing them to decide how far to go; (2) giving warmth, concern, and support when, and only when, it is genuinely felt; (3) gently confronting a participant when there are obvious discrepancies between her words and her behavior; and (4) encouraging people to be who they are without their masks and shields.

• She will need to be able to maintain focus in the group.

Openness (Eph. 4:15, 16)

• A group leader must be aware of herself, open to others in the group, open to new experiences, and open to life-styles and values that are different from her own.

• As the leader she needs to have an *attitude* of openness, not revealing every aspect of her personal life, but disclosing enough of herself to give participants a sense of who she is.

• A group leader needs to recognize her own weaknesses and not spend energy concealing them from others. A strong sense of awareness allows her to be vulnerable with the group.

Nondefensiveness (1 Pet. 5:5)

• A group leader needs to be secure in her leadership role. When negative feelings are expressed she must be able to explore them in a nondefensive manner.

Stamina (Eph. 6:10)

• A group leader needs physical and emotional stamina and the ability to withstand pressure and remain vitalized until the group sessions end.

• She must be aware of her own energy level, have outside sources of spiritual and emotional nourishment, and have realistic expectations for the group's progress.

Perspective (Prov. 3:5, 6)

• A group leader needs to cultivate a healthy perspective which allows her to enjoy humor and be comfortable with the release of it at appropriate times in a meeting.

• Although she will hear pain and suffering, she must trust the Lord to do the work and not take responsibility for what he alone can do.

• She needs to have a good sense of our human condition

and God's love, as well as a good sense of timing that allows her to trust the Holy Spirit to work in the women's lives.

Creativity (Phil. 1:9-11)

• She needs to be flexible and spontaneous, able to discover fresh ways to approach each session.

WHAT SPECIFIC SKILLS DOES A LEADER NEED?

A support group leader needs to be competent and comfortable with basic group communications skills. The following five are essential for healthy and open interaction:

Rephrase

• Paraphrase back to the speaker what you thought she said. Example: "I hear you saying that you felt. . . ."

Clarify

• To make sure you heard correctly ask the speaker to explain further. Example: "I'm not hearing exactly what you meant when you said. . . ."

Extend

• Encourage the speaker to be more specific. Example: "Can you give us an example. . . ."

Ask for Input

• Give the other women opportunity to share their opinions. Example: "Does anyone else have any insight on this?"

Be Personal and Specific

• Use women's names and convey "I" messages instead of "you" messages. "I'm feeling afraid of your reaction, " instead of "You scare me."

ADDITIONAL COMMUNICATION SKILLS

Active Listening

• A good listener learns to "hear" more than the words that are spoken. She absorbs the content, notes the gestures, the body language, the subtle changes in voice or expression, and senses the unspoken underlying messages.

• As a good listener, a leader will need to discern those in the group who need professional counseling and be willing to address this.

Empathy

• This requires sensing the subjective world of the participant—and caring. Of grasping another's experience and at the same time listening objectively.

Respect and Positive Regard

• In giving support, leaders need to draw on the positive assets of the members. Where differences occur, there needs to be open and honest appreciation and acceptance.

• Leaders must be able to maintain confidentiality and instill that emphasis in the group.

Expressing Warmth

• Smiling is especially important in communicating warmth to a group. Other nonverbal expressions are voice tone, posture, body language, and facial expression.

Genuineness

• Leaders need to be real, to be themselves in relating with others, to be authentic and spontaneous, to realize that the Holy Spirit works naturally.

WHAT DOES A LEADER ACTUALLY DO?

The leader will need to establish the atmosphere of the support group and show by her style how to relate lovingly and helpfully in the group. She needs to have God's heart for God's people. The following outline specific tasks.

She organizes logistics

• The leader helps arrange initial details of the early meetings—time, place, books, etc. (Note: Leaders need to be aware that much secular material, though good in information, is humanistic in application. "I" and "Self" are the primary focus, rather than Christ.)

She provides sense of purpose and vision

• She reminds the group of their purpose from time to time so that the group remains focused.

She acts as the initiator

• She makes sure everyone knows each other, helps them get acquainted and feel comfortable with each other. Makes sure meetings start and end on time.

She continues as an encourager to group members

• This basically means encouraging feelings to be expressed, keeping the atmosphere nonjudgmental and accepting, giving feedback, answering questions, clarifying things that were expressed, etc. Praying with and for members.

She sets expectations

• She models openness and interest in the group. She must be willing to take risks by resolving conflicts and clarifying intentions. She holds up standards of confidentiality personally and by reminding the group at each meeting. Confidentiality is crucial to the health of a group, and women should not divulge any private sharing, even to spouses, family, etc.

• She must be watchful and able to guide individuals away from destructive responses. Example: "I have a right to be hurt." She will need to always separate the person from her behavior, meeting the person where she is. Example: "We accept that you are hurt. Do you need to talk about it?"

She is sensitive to the Spirit

• She must know when someone needs to be referred to a professional counselor, pastor, etc., and be willing to work that problem through.

• She should be comfortable in ministering freely in the gifts of the Holy Spirit.

She gives the guidelines

• It is important that the women know the "ground rules." The leader needs to repeat these often, and *always* when newcomers attend. The following are basic support group guidelines:

1. You have come to give and receive support. No "fixing." We are to listen, support, and be supported by one another, not give advice.

2. Let other members talk. Please let them finish without interruption.

3. Try to step over any fear of sharing in the group. Yet do not monopolize the group's time.

4. Be interested in what someone else shares. Listen with your heart. Never converse privately with someone while another woman is talking or belittle her beliefs or expressions.

161

5. Be committed to express your feelings from the heart. Encourage others to do the same. It's all right to feel angry, to laugh, or to cry.

6. Help others own their feelings and take responsibility for change in their lives. Don't jump in with an easy answer or a story on how you conquered their problem or automatically give scripture as a "pat answer." Relate to where they are.

7. Avoid accusing or blaming. Speak in the "I" mode about how something or someone made you feel. Example: "I felt angry when. . . ."

8. Avoid ill-timed humor to lighten emotionally charged times. Let participants work through their sharing even if it is hard.

9. Keep names and sharing of other group members confidential.

10. Because we are all in various stages of growth, please give others permission to be where they are in their growth. This is a "safe place" for all to grow and share their lives.

She handles group discussion

Everyone is different. Your support group will have a variety of personalities. As a leader you will need to protect the group from problem behavior and help the individuals work through it. The following are examples of ways to help each person contribute so that the group benefits:

THEIR BEHAVIOR	YOUR ACTION
Too talkative	Interject by summarizing what the talker is saying. Turn to someone else in the group and redirect a question: "Elaine, what do you feel about that?"

A "fixer"	Show appreciation for their help and insight. Then direct a question to someone else. It is important to draw others in so that the woman needing help gets a healthy perspective on her situation and doesn't close off with a quickie solution.
Rambler	Thank them. If necessary, even break in, comment briefly, and move the discussion on.
Antagonist	Recognize legitimate objections when you can. Turn their comments to a constructive view. If all else fails, discuss the attitude privately and ask for their help.
Obstinate	Ask them to clarify. They may honestly not understand what you're talking about. Enlist others to help them see the point. If that doesn't work, tell them you will discuss the matter after the meeting.
Wrong topic	Focus on the subject. Say something such as: "Mary, that's interesting, but tonight we're talking about. . . ."
Her own problems	Bring it into the discussion if it is related. Otherwise, acknowledge

163

the problem and say: "Yes, I can see why that hurts you. Could we talk about it privately?"

Controversial questions	State clearly what you can or cannot discuss. Say something such as: "Problems do exist, but we do not discuss political issues here."
Side conversations	Stop and draw them into your discussion by asking for their ideas.
Personality clash	If a dispute erupts, cut across with a direct question on the topic. Bring others into the discussion: "Let's concentrate on the issue and not make this a personal thing."
Wrong choice of words	Point out that their idea is good and then help them by putting their idea into your words. Protect them from ridicule.
Definitely wrong	Make a clear comment, in an affirming way. "That's another point of view and of course you're entitled to your opinion." Then move on.
Bored	Try to find where their area of interest is. Draw them in to share their experience.

Question you can't answer	Redirect the question to the group. If you don't know the answer, say so and offer to find out.
Never participates	Use direct questions. Remind the group that they will get more out of the meeting when they open up.
Quiet, unsure of self	Affirm them in the eyes of the group. Ask direct questions you are sure they can answer.

She evaluates the meeting

• Support groups are a growing experience for everyone, including the leader. Don't be afraid to deal with habitual problems.

• Periodically involve the total group in evaluating how things are going.

She understands conflict and can handle it positively

• She understands the biblical pattern for making peace with our sisters in Christ. (See Matthew 5:9 and Romans 14:19.)

• She understands that Jesus has given us clear guidelines to resolve conflict and effect reconciliation and that our motive must be to demonstrate God's love, not vengeance. (See Matthew 5:23, 24 and Matthew 18:15-17.)

• She understands that we approach all situations humbly, knowing that none of us is without sin (Gal. 6:1-4) and that we are seeking reconciliation and forgiveness, not proving who is right and who is wrong.

• She avoids sermonizing.

• She knows that every group will experience conflict

on their way to becoming mature and effective, but uses it to help clarify goals and boundaries for the group.

- She defines and describes the conflict as "our group problem."
- She deals with issues rather than personalities.
- She takes one issue at a time.
- She tries to catch issues while they are small rather than letting them escalate over time.
- She invites cooperation, rather than intimidating or giving ultimatums.
- She expresses need for full disclosure of all the facts rather than allowing hidden agendas or leftover hurt feelings.
- She tries to maintain a friendly, trusting attitude.
- She recognizes others' feelings and concerns and opts for a "win-win" feeling rather than an "us and them" attitude.
- She encourages the expression of as many new ideas and as much new information as possible to broaden the perspective of all involved.
- She involves every woman in the conflict at a common meeting.
- She clarifies whether she is dealing with one conflict or several on-going ones.

She knows how to use feedback

Feedback helps another person get information on her behavior. It is essential in a support group to help the women keep on target and more effectively move through her problems.

- The group leader helps make feedback specific. Example: "Just now when we were talking about forgiveness, you changed the subject and started to blame your brother."

• She directs feedback toward behavior that the receiver can do something about. Example: "Would you like to make a choice to release your judgment against your friend?"

• She takes into account the needs of both the receiver and the giver of feedback. Feedback can be destructive if it's given to "straighten out" someone, rather than lovingly point out where that person is.

• She knows feedback is most useful when it is asked for. She can say: "Margaret, are you open to some feedback?"

• She watches for good timing. She tries to give feedback at the earliest opportunity after the given behavior occurs.

• She checks to ensure clear communication. One way of doing this is to have the receiver paraphrase the feedback to see if that is what the sender meant. Example: "I heard you saying that I need to examine my motives for. . . ."

ONE FINAL WORD

Be encouraged if the Lord has called you to be a support group leader or a member of a group. The Lord promises to do the work of healing, to be with us, to grant us patience, love, mercy—everything we need to follow his commission to love. There will be hard and even painful times. But we can count on him. "He who began a good work in you (in us) will carry it on to completion until the day of Christ Jesus" (Phil. 1:6).

OTHER BOOKS BY AGLOW PUBLICATIONS

Heart Issues

Stanley Baldwin   **If I'm Created in God's Image Why Does It Hurt to Look in the Mirror?**
A True View of You

Janet Bly   **Friends Forever**
The Art of Lifetime Relationships

Gloria Chisholm   **The Gift of Encouragement**
How to be a Warm Shoulder in a Cold World

Michelle Cresse   **Beyond Fear**
The Quantum Leap to Courageous Living

Jigsaw Families
Solving the Puzzle of Remarriage

Marilyn Fanning   **Compassionate Care**
Practical Love for Your Aging Parents

Denise George   A Longing Heart Hears **God's Gentle Whisper**

Heather Harpham   **Daddy, Where Were You?**
Healing for the Father-deprived Daughter

Diana Kruger	**Who Says Winners Never Lose?** Profiting from Life's Painful Detours
Pam Ravan	**Sock Hunting and Other Pursuits of the Working Mother**
Patricia Rushford	**Lost in the Money Maze?** How to Find Your Way Through
Marie Sontag	**When Love is Not Perfect** Discover God's Re-parenting Process

General Books

Barbara Cook	**Love and Its Counterfeits** **Romance** A God-given Experience of Beauty and Intimacy
Marion Duckworth	**What's Real Anyway?** Eternal Living in an Everyday World
Irene Endicott	**Grandparenting Redefined** Guidance for Today's Changing Family
Carol Greenwood	**A Rose for Nana** & Other Touches from an Everyday God

Jane Hansen with Carol Greenwood	**Inside a Woman** Revealing Her Longings, Pain, and the Journey to Love
Ranelda Mack Hunsicker	**Secrets** Unlocking the Mystery of Intimacy With God
Kathy Collard Miller	**Healing the Angry Heart** A Strategy for Confident Mothering
	Sure Footing in a Shaky World A Woman's Journey to Security
Jennie Newbrough	**Support Group Guide**
Quin Sherrer	**How to Pray for Your Children**
Quin Sherrer with Ruthanne Garlock	**How to Forgive Your Children**
Joanne Smith and Judy Biggs	**How to Say Goodbye** Working through Personal Grief
Pat Springle	**Codependency** Breaking Free from the Hurt and Manipulation of Dysfunctional Relationships (Word-Aglow special edition)

We at Aglow Publications encourage you to stop in at your Christian bookstore and pick up these books. If you do not have access to a Christian bookstore, you may order toll free at 1-800-755-2456.

Inquiries regarding speaking availability and other correspondence may be directed to Denise George at the following address:

c/o Beeson Divinity School
Samford University
Birmingham, AL 35229